LAW & ECONOMICS:
A CHRISTIAN PERSPECTIVE

Rodney D. Chrisman

λόγια

LOGIA PRESS, LLC

Forest, Virginia
2016

Published by Logia Press, LLC
Forest, Virginia 24551
orders@logiapress.com
First Edition: September 2016

For my wife and best friend, Heather,
and my children, Sierra, Alexis, Victoria,
Elijah, Samuel, Abraham,
Olivia, Averie, and Emarie.

"Logia" is the English transliteration of the Greek word "λόγια," which is translated "oracles." This word is used four times in the New Testament. Stephen uses this word in his famous speech in *Acts* 7:38 when he tells the audience that Moses "received the living oracles ["λόγια"] to give unto us." Paul uses it in *Romans* 3:2 when he notes of the Jews "that unto them were committed the oracles ["λόγια"] of God." Peter uses it when he writes that "[i]f any man speak, let him speak as the oracles ["λόγια"] of God." 1 *Peter* 4:11. Finally, the writer of Hebrews uses logia when he castigates his readers for their becoming dull of hearing and not progressing to being teachers as they ought have been by that time (*Hebrews* 5:12-14). He instead states that they needed someone to teach them "the first principles of the oracles ["λόγια"] of God." *Hebrews* 5:12.

In each of the passages, "logia" is used to refer to the authoritative pronouncements of the Lord God, including pronouncements in both the Old and New Testament eras. This word, and the corresponding belief that Scripture contains the authoritative pronouncements or logia of God for all areas of life, inspired the name of the publisher, Logia Press, LLC. God has spoken His logia. May his people seek to understand and apply His logia in every sphere of life, including law and policy, for His glory alone.

Logia Press, LLC
Forest, VA
September, 2016

The Purpose of the Book

As noted in the first chapter, this book is written to help students of the law consider the economic analysis of law, commonly referred to as law and economics, from a Christian perspective. It is certainly not complete. Much more could be said about every topic, and, for every topic, likely hundreds more could be considered. Thus, the hope is not a comprehensive Christian critique of law and economics (as laudable as that goal would be). Rather, what this book hopes to do is set forth a Christian understanding of law and compare and contrast it with the law and economics approach on a select number of issues and topics. I hope to do this in an interesting way that might equip students to continue the practice of the application of the Christian worldview to other issues that they encounter in law and policy and indeed in their lives in general. The Bible is authoritative for all things to which it speaks, and it speaks to all things, including issues of law and policy.

The Approach of this Book

With the broad purpose stated, I thought it appropriate to state a word about the approach of the book. One of things that I liked best about law school and the practice of law were the interesting cases. The facts of the cases that one encounters in practice and in law school are often very memorable. The writing of certain judges can also be engaging and fascinating. Therefore, I have chosen, for the most part, to structure this book, like the other Logia Press titles, around a number of carefully chosen cases and other materials that raise topics that I want us to think through together. I hope that you find the cases as interesting and enjoyable as I have.

The materials preceding and following the cases are designed to help you apply the Christian worldview to the issues presented. Sometimes I attempt a resolution of a particular issue. Other times I do not (or, perhaps, cannot.) The application of a biblical worldview to the complex legal and policy issues of our day is, to distort an old saying, a row that only a few are hoeing. Since few Christian scholars are working in this area in our time, the task to which we shall set ourselves in this book is made all the harder. But, perhaps as a result of this, any successes that God may grant us to enjoy may be all the sweeter.

Finally, as to the approach, I will also include questions that are meant to further stimulate your thought and possibly provide fodder for discussion. Sometimes these questions may cause us to reconsider items that have long been a part of the American legal and political systems. This can be somewhat uncomfortable. However, we should not shy away from this important work. Nothing, even by long use and custom, can become good if God's word condemns it.

A Word as to Judges, Authors, Cases, and Other Materials Cited

Lawyers cite and argue from authorities. Thus, a critical skill for a lawyer, and indeed any person, to develop is the ability to evaluate, distinguish, critique, and learn from various authorities. To that end, I cite a number of cases written by various judges, and I cite materials written by various authors, some of which I would agree with and some of which I would not.

Hopefully this will not be surprising. If this were a book about constitutional law, I would have you read *Roe v. Wade*. Certainly, writing from a Christian worldview, the fact that I would have you read that case would not cause you to draw the conclusion that I agree with everything in it. (The fact is that I agree with very little in it, and I think it is one of the most despicable opinions ever written.) We would read the case, not because we agree with it, but because we do not and it is a part of the legal (and indeed political) fabric of modern America. Many of the materials and authorities quoted, cited, and used in this book are selected for similar reasons.

Therefore, the inclusion of materials in this book, including the cases, should not be construed as an approval or endorsement of the judge, author, or arguments presented merely because of their inclusion in the text. Further, agreement with a judge or author on one point should not be construed as an endorsement of that author on all points. Rather, discernment is needed—and, in my opinion, required. You may not agree with me on all points, and likely you will not. Nor would I likely agree with you on all points. We should be able to state our arguments clearly and even forcefully to one another, and yet remain friends or colleagues. It seems to me that "love your neighbor" requires in this setting that we deal fairly with each argument offered, noting areas of agreement and disagreement, in a professional manner. Further, we should extend that same respect and love to the authors and judges whose materials are contained herein.

My Approach in Editing of Cases

I have edited the cases contained in this book. If you look these cases up in their full glory, you will likely want to write me and thank me for this.

Cases, particularly U.S. Supreme Court cases, tend to be bloated with argumentation and citations that are tedious even for lawyers to read. In fact, many modern Supreme Court cases seemed designed to weary the reader into submission as opposed to winning him over with persuasive argument. I have attempted to spare you the ordeal of being wearied by the sheer number of words alone.

Generally, I have followed the normal editing conventions, such as indicating deleted and inserted material. Deleted material I usually indicated with ellipses or ***. Inserted material is set apart in brackets. Footnotes are often deleted without any indication, as are most citations to other authorities. When footnotes are included, they are typically renumbered in conformity with the numbering used in the book. At times minor corrections, additions, and changes have been made without any indication whatsoever. Further, many grammatical and some spelling errors are left in the cases as they appear in the originals. Language changes over time, and court opinions are no exceptions. Of course, if you have questions about what has been deleted or added, I would direct you to the actual opinions for comparison, as they are freely available from a number of sources on the Internet.

Acknowledgments and Thanks

As always, I would like to thank my lovely bride, Heather, for her love, companionship, support, ideas, suggestions, and editing assistance. I could not begin to express how much she means to me and how indebted I am to her. Her worth is indeed far above rubies, and she does me good and not evil all the days of my life. *Proverbs* 31:10-12.

I would also like to express my gratitude to Dean Jeffrey S. Tuomala and the late Professor Roger Bern for granting me permission to use and quote extensively from their excellent articles: Jeffrey S. Tuomala, Marbury v. Madison *and the Foundation of Law*, 4 Liberty U. L. Rev. 297 (2010); and Roger Bern, *A Biblical Model for Analysis of Issues of Law and Public Policy: With Illustrative Applications to Contracts, Antitrust, Remedies, and Public Policy Issues*, 6 Regent U. L. Rev. 103 (1995).

Obviously, all the mistakes, whether grammatical, typographical, conceptual, or otherwise, remain my own.

And, last but not least, I thank you for reading and studying the book. I hope you grow in your understanding of and love for the law and, more importantly, the Lord whose righteous standard it represents. May He soon establish His justice on the earth and the distant lands hope in His law. *Isaiah* 42:4.

Soli Deo Gloria

Rodney D. Chrisman
Forest, VA
September, 2016

TABLE OF CONTENTS

CHAPTER 1
INTRODUCTION

The purpose of this book is to consider the economic analysis of issues of law and policy, commonly referred to as law and economics, from a Christian perspective. Given the prevalence and importance of law and economics to modern jurisprudence, this is a daunting challenge. Law and economics thinking has reached deep into virtually every corner of American law. Accordingly, a full treatment of every topic addressed by law and economics scholarship, or even just all of the topics addressed in Judge Richard Posner's book *Economic Analysis of Law*, is beyond the scope of this present work.

Rather, what this book hopes to do is set forth a Christian understanding of law and compare and contrast it with the law and economics approach. This will be accomplished, if it is accomplished at all, the way I do it in the classroom when I teach law and economics—by covering a number of topics, cases, and issues; discussing the law and economics approach to those topics, cases, and issues; discussing a Christian approach to the same; and then comparing and contrasting the law and economics approach with the Christian approach.

As we attempt to do this together in this book, I am assuming that you have some edition of Judge Posner's *Economic Analysis of Law* that you are using in addition to this book. Rather than trying to restate the position of law and economics scholars on each and every issue that I address, I prefer for you to read the law and economics position as stated by its most gifted and prolific apologist, Judge Posner.[1]

To begin, this chapter serves as an introduction to both law and economics and a Christian approach to law. It attempts to set out, in relatively basic terms, the fundamental tenets of both the law and economics and Christian approaches to issues of law and policy. The following chapters expound upon this by considering topics, issues, and cases from a number of areas of law such as property, contracts, torts, criminal, bankruptcy, and corporate law, to name a few. Let's get started by taking a look at the

---

[1] Judge Richard A. Posner has served on the U.S. Court of Appeals for the Seventh Circuit since 1981. He also teaches as the University of Chicago Law School. He is an absolutely prolific writer. For more information on Judge Posner, see his faculty page on the University of Chicago Law School's website here: http://www.law.uchicago.edu/faculty/posner-r (last visited August 25, 2016).

importance of law and economics in our time and recognizing the resultant need for a Christian response.

I. *The Influence of Law and Economics, the Myth of Neutrality, and the Necessity of a Christian Response*

Law and economics is the most influential jurisprudential thought system of our time. In the preface to his immensely popular and influential "textbook-treatise" on law and economics entitled *Economic Analysis of Law*, Judge Posner asserts that law and economics "is the foremost interdisciplinary field of legal studies."[2] In support of this statement, he writes:

> The former dean of the Yale Law School, a critic of the law and economics movement, nevertheless has called it "an enormous enlivening force in American legal thought" and says that it "continues and remains the single most influential jurisprudential school in this country." More recently we read that "there is no dispute that law and economics has long been, and continues to be, the dominant theoretical paradigm for understanding and assessing law and policy."[3]

Further, Brian Bix accurately notes the enormous influence of law and economics on the American legal system. He writes:

> In the United States, no approach to law in recent decades has been more influential than the economic analysis of law (also known by the shorthand, "law and economics"); it dominates thinking about antitrust law, tort law, and most commercial law areas. Even areas which would seem uncongenial to economic analysis . . . have had significant contributions from attempts to apply this approach. There seem to be no domains free from attempts to apply this approach.[4]

Bix continues:

> The current influence of law and economics can be seen in the way that even those highly critical of that approach use its terminology and respond to the issues it raises. There is a sense in which law and economics now sets the agenda, or at

---

[2] Richard A. Posner, *Economic Analysis of Law* xxi (8th ed. 2011).

[3] *Id.* (footnotes omitted) (citing and quoting Anthony T. Kronman, *Remarks at the Second Driker Forum for Excellence in the Law*, 42 Wayne L. Rev. 115, 144 and 160 (1995) and Jon Hanson and David Yosifson, *The Situation: An Introduction to the Situational Character, Critical Realism, Power Economics, and Deep Capture*, 152 U. Pa. L. Rev. 129, 142 (2003)).

[4] Brian Bix, *Jurisprudence: Theory and Context* 201 (5th ed. 2009).

least offers the initial framework, for most discussions of policy and reform in American academic, legal, and political debate.[5]

Obviously, such an influential thought system is one that Christian legal professionals, and indeed Christian citizens, must understand and to which we must be able to make a response.

Many explanations for why law and economics has become so influential and widely accepted in our times could be suggested. Certainly the brilliance and amazing productivity of its chief proponent, Judge Posner, plays a large role. Judge Posner is a true polymath, and his immense intelligence and tireless advocacy of law and economics has undoubtedly done much to aid its rise.

Another likely reason is that law and economics has had a huge impact on the way law is taught, and, by impacting how law is taught for a number of decades, it has managed to dramatically impact how at least a generation of lawyers think about and approach the law. Judge Posner explains his view of the reason for this in the Preface to the Ninth Edition of *Economic Analysis of Law*.

> The reason [that law and economics has changed the way law is taught] has to do with the extreme surface complexity of the law. The law is divided into numerous fields, each with its own complex structure of rules. The fields are traditionally studied in isolation from one another, and within each field the rules tend also to be studied as separate, often self-enclosed, bodies of thought. Yet a relative handful of economic doctrines . . . can, by their repeated application across fields of law and legal rules, describe a great deal of the legal system and enable the student to develop a more coherent sense of the system—to grasp the relation of its parts and understand its essential unity, and having done so to deal competently with new issues as they arise.[6]

This is a laudable goal, and it is one that I share with Judge Posner in that I, too, would like to help reduce the complexity of law for my students thereby enabling them to better grasp the law as a whole, a *corpus juris* if you will, and "to competently deal with new issues as they arise." The law in our time has become enormously complex and technical such that it can feel as if there are no unifying principles, no way to understand or make sense of the whole, and no way to be competent in more than one small area of it. This is dispiriting to law students, lawyers, judges, and indeed the citizenry as a whole. As a third-year law student taking law and economics at the University of Kentucky College of Law, I found the economic analysis of law to be

---

[5] *Id.*, at 202.
[6] Richard A. Posner, *Economic Analysis of Law* xxi (9th ed. 2014).

extremely alluring and satisfying for this very reason—it seemed to provide this framework and coherence for the law that I had very much found missing in my studies of the law up to that point. Thus, I wholeheartedly agree with the goal.

However, while Judge Posner and I agree on the goal—reducing the complexity of law by identifying essential unities therein such that it can be better understood as a *corpus juris*, we disagree rather markedly on how it is to be accomplished. For all the promise of law and economics on this front, and despite my initial affinity for it, I am convinced it cannot deliver. Rather, if this goal is to be accomplished at all, it must be accomplished in the way it was in the historic Western legal tradition—by reference to the Christian worldview and a law of nature and nature's God approach that is faithful thereto.[7]

In addition to these reasons, law and economics has become so influential and widely accepted in our times because it seeks to avoid what Judge Posner would call "controversial metaphysical commitments."[8] For example, my belief that Jesus Christ is the sovereign Lord of the universe and that He can, by right, demand the obedience of every person and every nation on earth is definitely a controversial metaphysical commitment, according to Judge Posner.[9] As a derivative of this belief, I also believe that Jesus Christ's revelation of His righteous standards is binding on all people in all places throughout all time. Of course, this is another controversial metaphysical commitment. It is a belief that there are answers to the "big questions" (metaphysical questions) in life, such as: Is there a God? Why am I here? Is there life after death? Is the law real in some sense? Does a law above the law exist?

To be fair to Judge Posner, in this regard, he is merely a product of his time. Modern people are hostile to metanarratives or big stories that explain everything and answer the "big questions." Reality is thought to have no

---

[7] For example, the Puritan legal scholar Matthew Hale was purportedly able to draw on a large sheet of paper "a scheme of the whole order and parts of [the common law] to the great satisfaction of" some who had indicated that they "looked on the common law as a study that could not be brought into a scheme, nor formed into a rational science, by reason of the indigestedness of it, and the multiplicity of cases in it." William S. Holdsworth, *A History of English Law* (13 vols.) 6: 584 (1922-1952), cited and quoted by Harold J. Berman, *Law and Revolution II: The Impact of the Protestant Reformations on the Western Legal Tradition* 468 (2003).

[8] Richard A. Posner, *The Problematics of Moral and Legal Theory* 15 (1999). For more on Judge Posner's views on this topic and some response of my own, *see* Rodney D. Chrisman, *Why I can't conceivably influence the modern secular courts, at least according to Judge Posner.*, www.RodneyChrisman.com (Jan. 13, 2011), http://www.rodneychrisman.com/2011/01/13/why-i-cant-conceivably-influence-the-modern-secular-courts-at-least-according-to-judge-posner/.

[9] Posner, *Problematics* 15. Judge Posner writes that "[t]he Jesus Christ of the Gospels is a moralist, but, unlike Plato or Aquinas, he is not a theorist and does not make academic-style arguments. My concern is with the type of moralizing that is or at least pretends to be free from controversial metaphysical commitments, such as those of a believing Christian, and so might conceivably appeal to the judges of our secular courts." Obviously, my statements made herein, in the opinion of Judge Posner, could not conceivably appeal to our modern secular courts because they are indeed based upon "controversial metaphysical commitments."

ultimate meaning, and therefore a legal system cannot be influenced by or have any ultimate meaning or purpose. Accordingly, it is not necessarily that Judge Posner (and other modern thinkers) simply deny these things. Of course they do often deny them—but, more tellingly, modern people in general, and law and economics scholars like Judge Posner in particular, assert that these questions and their possible answers should not be a part of the legal discourse at all.[10] Instead, they argue that the legal system should be neutral, secular, and free from the bias and conflict that they would say comes from these controversial metaphysical commitments.

The problem is that neutrality like this is a myth. Just like me, you, and everyone else, Judge Posner operates out of his own metaphysical commitments, or we might say he operates out of his own worldview. In fact, it is impossible not to. We all see and understand the world through a particular set of assumptions about what is true and not true about the nature of things. In other words, it is impossible to be neutral. Accordingly, neutrality in law is no more possible than neutrality is in any other part of life.

Rejecting the purported neutrality in the realm of education, Dr. R. J. Rushdoony's thoughts are very helpful on this issue of neutrality. He writes:

> The idea of neutrality is, however, a myth. Every person and institution has a perspective and a plan which involves a commitment. If God is indeed the Creator of heaven and earth, and if the God of Scripture is the living God, to eliminate Him from education is not neutrality but enmity; the most important consideration of all is not considered. No man can be neutral towards God. The idea of neutrality presupposes an objectivity on the part of man which is not tenable. Moreover, we cannot assume that neutrality is essential to establishing truth; if a man is neutral towards all things, then all things are equally meaningless to him. Not even God professes to be neutral; He speaks of *hating* certain things and persons (e.g., Prov. 6:16–19). . . . Courts of law are not neutral; in a murder trial, neither the court nor the law is neutral about murder. Rather, the quest is for *justice* in procedure and judgment, something very different from neutrality.[11]

Further, noting that Cornelius Van Til denied the concept of neutrality, Dr. Rushdoony wrote "There are no neutral facts, no neutral thoughts, no neutral man nor reason. All men, facts, and thinking either begin with the sovereign and triune God, or they begin with rebellion against Him."[12]

---

[10] For an excellent discussion of the inadmissibility of religious categories and suppositions in modern legal thought, *see* Steven D. Smith, *Law's Quandary* 22-37 (2004).

[11] R. J. Rushdoony, *Sovereignty* 225–226 (2007) (emphasis in original).

[12] R. J. Rushdoony, *Systematic Theology in Two Volumes: Volume I* 60 (1994).

Neutrality being impossible, and everything either being in submission to God or in rebellion against Him (remember it was Jesus who said "he that is not with me is against me" in *Matthew* 12:30,) points to the reality that everything, including law, is at its base religious and theological.[13] Applying this to law, Dr. Rushdoony wrote:

> Law is in every culture *religious in origin*. Because law governs man and society, because it establishes and declares the meaning of justice and righteousness, law is inescapably religious, in that it establishes in practical fashion the ultimate concerns of a culture. Accordingly, a fundamental and necessary premise in any and every study of law must be, *first*, a recognition of this religious nature of law.
>
> *Second*, it must be recognized that in any culture *the source of law is the god of that society*. If law has its source in man's reason, then reason is the god of that society. If the source is an oligarchy, or in a court, senate, or ruler, then that source is the god of that system. Thus, in Greek culture law was essentially a religiously humanistic concept.
>
> . . .
>
> Modern humanism, the religion of the state, locates law in the state and thus makes the state, or the people as they find expression in the state, the god of the system. As Mao Tse-Tung has said, "Our God is none other than the masses of the Chinese people." In Western culture, law has steadily moved away from God to the people (or the state) as its source, although the historic power and vitality of the West has been in Biblical faith and law.[14]

The God of our legal system used to be the God of *The Bible*. Now, unfortunately, it is the state, or the civil magistrate, and this transition has been cloaked in a claim of neutrality cleverly designed to drive all viewpoints, except the secular humanist viewpoint, out of the law and out of the public square.

Judge Posner and other law and economics scholars, operating from a position of supposed and self-declared neutrality, posit that economic analysis, instead of a moral standard ultimately anchored in the God of *The Bible*, should be the guiding principle for law and policy in America. Further, they argue that this is really what judges have been doing all along anyway— seeking economic efficiency in order to increase societal wealth. In fact,

---

[13] *See, e.g.,* Rodney D. Chrisman, *The Law is Inescapably Theological (Just Like the Rest of Life),* www.RodneyChrisman.com (August 13, 2010), http://www.rodneychrisman.com/2010/08/13/the-law-is-inescapably-theological-just-like-the-rest-of-life/.

[14] R. J. Rushdoony, *The Institutes of Biblical Law, Volume One* 4-5 (1973) (quoting Mao Tse-Tung, *The Foolish Old Man Who Removed Mountains* 3 (1966)) (emphasis in original).

according to law and economics, the goal of the legal system should be to facilitate (and not unnecessarily impede) the flow of societal resources to those users who value them most, thereby maximizing and increasing societal wealth. The best way to accomplish this is generally considered to be through the market.

This is a very appealing proposition. After all, can't we all agree that society being wealthier is a good thing? Isn't it a worthy goal to find some guiding principle around which we can all "just get along?" Perhaps, but we have to remember the earlier discussion about law being inexorably tied to religion and theology.

Conservative Christians may often find themselves in agreement with law and economics scholars on many issues. However, we should avoid being seduced by this. When we agree, we often agree for very, very different reasons. We may agree on some particular fact, but the principles that lead us to this conclusion are far from one another. For example, many conservative Christians agree that the market is a good thing and that we do want resources in the hands of people who will use them most efficiently, just like many law and economics scholars. However, we don't reach this conclusion because we believe that the maximization of societal wealth is the greatest good and should be the guiding principle of law and policy. Rather, we reach this conclusion because God, as the Creator of the world, chose to entrust all of His creation to mankind, and we are therefore stewards with a duty to manage everything that God has entrusted to us in an efficient and non-wasteful manner. Some of the conclusions are the same, but the ultimate principles are very different.[15]

While many times there may be agreement on the particulars, as earlier noted, there is rarely agreement on the principles or generals. These differences on the principles are profound, and they can lead to startlingly different outcomes in many instances, as we shall see in this book. Therefore, it is critical that Christians have a response to the economic analysis of law. It is the duty of Christians "to destroy arguments and every lofty opinion raised against the knowledge of God, and take every thought captive to obey Christ,"[16] and, in the area of law, there is no more lofty opinion or argument raised up against the knowledge of God.

However, beyond the differing outcomes mentioned above, something even more important and fundamental to society is at stake. Without being overly dramatic, what is at stake is nothing less than the Western legal tradition itself, and the society with its unprecedented blessings of prosperity and liberty that the Western legal tradition has brought with it. As Harold J. Berman pointed out in his excellent work *Law and Revolution: The Formation of the Western Legal Tradition*, "[a]lmost all the nations of the West are threatened today by a cynicism about law, leading to a contempt for law, on

---

[15] For an interesting critique of law and economics by a Christian economics professor who teaches at the University of Virginia, *see* Kenneth G. Elzinga, *Law and Economics: Is there a Higher Law?*, 36 Pepp. L. Rev. 507 (2009).

[16] 2 Corinthians 10:5 (ESV).

the part of all classes of the population."[17]   This cynicism about the law and contempt for the law is an existential crisis for our civilization. As Professor Berman accurately noted in 1983, Western civilization and society has proved very resilient and has accommodated many ideas, changes, and upheavals, "[b]ut the disintegration of the very foundations of that tradition cannot be accommodated; and the greatest challenge to those foundations is the massive loss of confidence in the West itself, as a civilization, a community, and in the legal tradition which for nine centuries has helped to sustain it."[18]

Why do we see such a loss of confidence in the West itself? Why do people find themselves with so little faith in the law in our times? Why do we see this cynicism and contempt for law? A shift in the way that we as a society think, approach, and talk about the law is the reason. This began long before law and economics with Christopher Columbus Langdell and the rejection of the historic natural law view followed by Oliver Wendell Holmes and the American Legal Realists and their rejection of both the historic natural law position and formalism in legal reasoning.[19] Law and economics is merely the most sophisticated manifestation of this long trend that rejects the foundational principles upon which the Western legal tradition was based. Of this, Professor Berman writes:

> [The] basic institutions, concepts, and values of Western legal systems have their sources in religious rituals, liturgies, and doctrines of the eleventh and twelfth centuries, reflecting new attitudes toward death, sin, punishment, forgiveness, and salvation, as well as new assumptions concerning the relationship of the divine to the human and of faith to reason. Over the intervening centuries, these religious attitudes and assumptions have changed fundamentally, and today their theological sources seem to be in the process of drying up. Yet the legal institutions, concepts, and values that have derived from them still survive, often unchanged. Western legal science is a secular theology, which often makes no sense because its theological presuppositions are no longer accepted.
>
>   * * *
>
> [T]he legal systems of all Western countries, and of all non-Western countries that have come under the influence of Western law, are a secular residue of religious attitudes and assumptions which historically found expression first in the liturgy and rituals and doctrine of the church and thereafter in the institutions and concepts and values of the law. When

---

[17] Harold J. Berman, *Law and Revolution: The Formation of the Western Legal Tradition* 40 (1983).

[18] *Id.*

[19] *See, e.g.,* Albert W. Alschuler, *From Blackstone to Holmes: The Revolt Against Natural Law*, 36 Pepp. L. Rev. 491 (2009) and Herbert W. Titus, *God, Man, and Law: The Biblical Principles* 1-7 (1994).

these historical roots are not understood, many parts of the law
appear to lack any underlying source of validity.[20]

Without its historic foundations, the law lacks validity and naturally becomes
an object of cynicism and contempt.

Law and economics holds as a central tenant its rejection of these
historic foundations of law. It rejects any idea of a higher law or a law above
the law. It attempts to "do law" without reference to any sort of theological
presuppositions. But, this goal of understanding the *corpus juris* without
reference to and some margin of commitment to its historic roots is doomed to
fail, and this failure will ultimately take down the whole of the Western legal
tradition. Faced with such an existential threat, a Christian answer made in
fidelity to the religious attitudes and assumptions that gave rise to the
Western legal tradition is necessary for its salvation and ongoing development.
Certainly such a goal is too lofty for this small work, but, by the grace of God,
it may make some contribution in that direction.

II. *A Straightforward Introduction to Law and Economics Reasoning*

When trying to understand something, it is often helpful to start by
answering the question: what is the purpose or goal of this particular thing?
This is the approach taken by the *Westminster Shorter Catechism* when it asks
in the very first question: "What is the chief end of man?"[21] If we hope to
understand mankind, we should probably start by asking what is the goal,
purpose, or "chief end" of mankind. The *Catechism* answers that "Man's chief
end is to glorify God, (1 Cor. 10:31, Rom. 11:36) and to enjoy him forever (Ps.
73:25–28)."[22] Every other question and answer follows from that.

In this same vein, I will begin my attempt at a straightforward
introduction to law and economics reasoning by asking the question: what is
the goal or purpose of law and economics? Or, perhaps more clearly stated,
what goal does law and economics assume the law (and presumably society in
general) should pursue? The answer to that is clearly the maximization of
societal wealth.

How is this goal to be accomplished? According to law and economics,
societal wealth is maximized when the scarce resources belonging to or
available to a society are put into the hands of the people who can and will put
them to their highest and best use. When this happens, the resources are said
to be efficiently deployed and society's wealth will be maximized.

How do we know when resources have been efficiently deployed? How
do we know that they are in the hands of the people who can and will put them
to their highest and best use? To state it technically, we know that we have

---

[20] Berman, *Law and Revolution* 165-166.
[21] Westminster Assembly, *The Westminster Shorter Catechism: With Scripture Proofs*
(3rd ed. 1996).
[22] *Id.*

reached an efficient deployment of resources when no reallocation would increase value. To state it simply, when the resources have come to rest in the hands of the people who value them the most.

That, of course, begs the next question: how do we know whether a particular person is the person who values a particular resource the most? Several answers could be put forth here. Perhaps it could be the person who wants or needs it the most. Maybe it should be the person who would get the most happiness from possessing it. These questions present obvious problems of quantification. How do we know who wants or needs something the most? How do we measure that? How do we determine relative happiness? In an attempt to avoid these quantification problems, law and economics posits that the person who is willing and able to pay the most for a particular resource is the person who values it the most and therefore the person who will put it to the highest and best use thereby maximizing society's wealth.

Perhaps a quick example would be helpful here. Let's assume that I have an extra copy of Judge Posner's book that I am willing to sell for $50 and that there is a student in my Law and Economics course at the Law School who would like to purchase that book for $50. Let's assume that the next cheapest copy of the book that he can find is selling for $75 online. He is willing to pay any amount up to $75 for the book. I have two copies of the book, and, while I might be glad to have one copy at the office and one at home, I value that slight convenience less than I value $50 in cash.

If we engage in the hypothetical transaction, I am made better off because I value $50 (and presumably what it will buy me in other goods and services) more than I value the book, and the student values the book more than he values $50. Thus, after the transaction, the book is in the hand of someone who values it more (and perhaps most) because it is in the hands of the student, and I have the $50, which I value more. We are both better off or "wealthier," and that slightly increases the wealth of society as a whole.

In other words, the best way to get resources into the hands of people who value them the most is through voluntary transactions conducted in a free market with low or no transaction costs and limited third party effects. When people voluntarily part with resources in exchange for money or voluntarily part with money in exchange for resources, we can feel sure that the resources have moved into the hands of the person who values them the most, again, assuming that we mean by "values them the most" that he is willing and able to pay the most for them.

Accordingly, a big part of law and economics reasoning involves legal rules and policies that help to create and sustain an environment in which these types of voluntary exchanges flourish. But, unfortunately, the legal system is very often concerned with *involuntary* transactions such as crimes, accidents, regulations (health, safety, environmental, etc.), and imminent domain, among many others. In these involuntary transactions, how are we to determine whether we are efficiently deploying society's scarce resources? How are we to determine whether resources have moved into the hands of the person who values them the most and that they have therefore been put to their highest and best uses?

The answer is found in trying to mimic the market. Just as it was popular for a period of time for Christians to wear bracelets and other items bearing the letters WWJD (What would Jesus do?), a dedicated law and economics scholar might prefer WWMD (What would the market do?) In order to arrive at an efficient outcome in an involuntary setting, the decision maker should try to imagine what would be done in a hypothetical market transaction, if such a transaction could occur, and approximate that in the involuntary transaction to the greatest extent possible.

Obviously, there is a lot more to law and economics, but this does provide an overview that tends to guide all economic analysis of law. It is a quest for efficiency. It seeks to both explain the law as it is and historically has been and shape the law in the future by reference to this quest for efficiency. As a Christian, I am not at all opposed to efficiency, the market, etc. However, due to my "controversial metaphysical commitments," I know that there is much more to law, society, and indeed reality than just these things.

III. A Brief Introduction to a Christian Approach to Law

A Christian approach to law, by contrast, has as its purpose the glory of God. God is glorified through the law and the legal system by its reflection of His justice and His holy and righteous character, which is revealed in the law of nature and nature's God.

We will consider this approach to law in much more depth as we move through the book. For instance, in the coming chapters, you will consider specific applications of the three major issues that appear over and over again when considering a Christian worldview of law: jurisdiction, reasoning from general to particulars, and judicial as contrasted with prudential reasoning.

First, jurisdiction comes from the Latin words *juris* meaning law and *dictio* meaning to speak. Thus, literally, jurisdiction means the power to speak the law in a given area. Jurisdiction therefore is intimately related to authority. It is always important with any question of law and policy (and indeed most questions in all of life) to ask "who has the proper biblical authority to act here?" In our times virtually no one is asking this question anymore. Rather, the civil government, or the civil magistrate, has assumed virtually unlimited jurisdiction to itself attempting to act or assume authority or "speak the law" in every area of life. However, only the Lord Jesus Christ has such universal authority, and He will suffer no competitors.

Contrary to the spirit of times, Christians should always be asking who has authority to act and should assume that everyone and every institution has a limited authority except the Lord Jesus Christ. Accordingly, it might be that a certain problem is not within the jurisdiction of the civil magistrate, but perhaps the church, the family, the individual, or maybe that jurisdiction has been limited to God alone. How do we answer this question of who has authority or jurisdiction to act? By looking to the law of nature and nature's

God found in God's revelation of Himself in His world and most principly and specifically in *The Bible*.

Law and economics, you will find, has really no boundary or jurisdictional principles of any meaningful kind. All that is needed to trigger the jurisdiction of the civil magistrate in a law and economics system is a market failure impeding efficiency. If the market can't act properly in the judgement of the law and economics scholar, then the civil government should act, and these actions will not be bound by jurisdiction nor any overarching general principles of morality, etc., since, in a law and economics worldview, these broad general principles don't exist.

Second, and related thereto, a Christian approach to law is very much concerned with reasoning from generals to particulars. We do this in all of life. God has revealed to us both broad general principles (such as love God and love your neighbor) and narrow particulars (such as the penalty of restitution of four sheep for one stolen sheep.) We are required to reason from these general principles down to particular situations. (And, sometimes, from particular specifics up to generals as well.) This is a big part of what the law is all about— ascertaining the proper general principles of law and applying those generals properly in given particular situations.

Law and economics eschews all broad general principles, especially moral general principles, except for the maximization of societal wealth. This, for a law and economics scholar, is the great general principle and, for the most part, there are no others. Thus, law and policy reasoning frequently devolves to using social science to attempt to determine what is efficient in any given situation and then implementing that. A biblical system, by contrast, has a wealth of general principles found in the law of nature and nature's God, and these general principles should then be reasoned from to answer various questions of law and policy.

Third, when considering issues of law and policy, it is very important to consider what type of reasoning should be applied based upon the role in which one is acting. A judge should reason like a judge, and a legislator should reason like a legislator. Both do this subject to the law of nature and nature's God, but part of that means understanding of and discipline in how to reason. A judge reasons by looking back, ascertaining a standard, and applying it to a set of facts. A judge should not reason prospectively, but retrospectively, in most cases. By contrast, a legislator should reason prospectively, looking forward and asking what is prudent.

Law and economics completely rejects this distinction. Law and economics, like American legal realism, calls upon judges to abandon traditional legal reasoning in favor of prudential reasoning. However, as we shall see, this is destructive to a legal system based upon the rule of law and eventually undermines faith in the judiciary and the legal system as a whole.

For additional reading that would help you begin to learn and apply a distinctly Christian approach to law, I would strongly recommend that you read these three articles: Jeffrey Tuomala, Marbury v. Madison *and the Foundation of Law*, 4 Liberty U. L. Rev. 297 (2010); Roger Bern, *A Biblical Model for Analysis of*

Issues of Law and Public Policy: With Illustrative Applications to Contracts, Antitrust, Remedies, and Public Policy Issues, 6 Regent U. L. Rev. 103 (1995); and Rodney D. Chrisman, Rodney D. Chrisman, *Can a Merchant Please God?: The Church's Historic Teaching on the Goodness of Just Commercial Activity as a Foundational Principle of Commercial Law Jurisprudence,* 6 Liberty U. L. Rev. 453 (2012). These articles are long and academic in nature, but they represent a wealth of what it means to approach issues of law and policy in a manner that is honoring and glorifying to the Lord, and I believe you will find them most helpful.

Private property rights and the law governing those private property rights are critical to developed society and its legal system. In fact, private property ownership has been found to be a critical factor in determining whether a nation will be wealthy or impoverished.[23] On this, law and economics and the Christian worldview of law agree. However, as the following discussion demonstrates, this agreement on the particular of the importance and necessity of private property rights and their protection by law is derived from very different general principles.

I. The Justification for and Source of Private Property Rights

Law and economics scholars seem to offer only the inefficiency of the alternative as their justification for private property rights. Judge Posner gives an example of a farmer being unwilling to make the investment in planting and cultivating crops if there were no property rights because, absent successful defensive measures, others would just take the fruits of his labors without consequence. He rightly notes that "the cultivation of land will be abandoned after a few such incidents of unauthorized taking and society will shift to methods of subsistence (such as hunting) that involve less preparatory investment."[24] Accordingly, without private property rights, society will operate less efficiency and be less wealthy and therefore a legal system should provide for and protect private property rights.

Given this justification for private property rights and the aversion of most law and economics scholars to metaphysical questions, it is not surprising that the source of private property rights is likely to be seen as going no higher than the civil government. Judge Posner's discussion of property law nowhere includes a discussion of ultimate property ownership or any type of transcendental source of private property rights. Rather, the discussion

---

[23] *See, e.g.,* Wayne Grudem and Barry Asmus, *The Poverty of Nations: A Sustainable Solution* 141-154 (2013).

[24] Posner, *Economic Analysis of Law* 40 (9th ed. 2014). Judge Posner also demonstrates this in static analysis with the example of the common pasture, which he asserts is also less efficient than private ownership. *Id.* at 40-41.

demonstrates that the civil government is the source of private property rights, in the sense that there is no higher source, and that it is up to the civil government, through its various branches and agencies, to make rules for the efficient assignment of property rights.[25]

The Christian view of the justification for private property rights and their ultimate source is quite different. According to a Christian worldview, God created private property rights, which should clearly be understood as a good gift from Him. God is therefore the source of private property rights. The justification for their existence, accordingly, is found in obedience to God's commands as found in *The Bible*, which clearly teaches the concept of private property ownership.

For this, one need look no further than the Eighth Commandment, "You shall not steal."[26] If there were no concept of the private ownership of property, there would be no need for a commandment against stealing. How would you know if someone stole your laptop if there was no concept of it actually being *your* laptop?

This should not be understood to deny God as the ultimate owner of all things as many passages clearly demonstrate the contrary. For example, *Psalm* 24:1-2 says "The earth is the Lord's and the fullness thereof, the world and those who dwell therein, for he had founded it upon the seas and established it upon the rivers."[27] God is the ultimate owner of all things because He is the Creator of all things. He made the universe, and He is the ultimate owner of everything in it.

Therefore, rightly understood, humans are stewards of God's creation, granted by Him a sort of vice-regency and an accompanying temporal ownership of property. Genesis 1:28 contains this initial grant to the first man and all of his descendants. "And God blessed them. And God said to them, 'Be fruitful and multiply and fill the earth and subdue it and have dominion over the fish of the sea and over the birds of the heavens and over every living thing that moves on the earth." Thus, human property rights are derived from God and temporal in nature, but they are property rights none the less.

In *The Institutes of Biblical Law*, R. J. Rushdoony comments on this issue in the context of discussing the Eighth Commandment. He writes:

> It is very necessary . . . to recognize that the urge to dominion is God-given and is basic to the nature of man. An aspect of this dominion is property.
>
>   * * *
>
> The earth is indeed the Lord's, as is all dominion, but God has chosen to give dominion over the earth to man, subject to His law-word, and property is a central aspect of dominion.

---

[25] Posner, *Economic Analysis of Law* 39-91 (9th ed. 2014).
[26] Exodus 20:15 and Deuteronomy 5:19 (ESV).
[27] *See also* Psalms 50:10-11, 89:11.

The absolute and transcendental title to property is the Lord's; the present and historical title to property is man's.   . . .

The Scripture, however, places property in the hands of the family, not the state. It gives property to man as an aspect of his dominion, as a part of his godly subduing of the earth.[28]

Wayne Grudem puts it somewhat differently, but he still seems to agree. In his excellent little book *Business for the Glory of God: The Bible's Teaching on the Moral Goodness of Business*, he writes this of ownership:

I believe the reason God gave the command, "You shall not steal," is that ownership of possessions is a fundamental way that we imitate God's sovereignty over the universe by our exercising "sovereignty" over a tiny portion of the universe, things we own. When we take care of our possessions, we imitate God in his taking care of the whole universe, and he delights to see us imitate him in this way. In addition, when we care for our possessions, it gives us opportunity to imitate many other attributes of God, such as wisdom, knowledge, beauty, creativity, love for others, kindness, fairness, independence, freedom, exercise of will, blessedness (or joy), and so forth.

* * *

Why do children from a very early age enjoy having toys that are their own, and why do they often want to have a pet that is their own, one they can care for? I realize that such "ownership" of toys and pets can be distorted by the sins of selfishness and laziness, but even if we lived in a sinless world children from a very young age would have a desire to have things that are their own. I think God has created us with a desire to own things because he wanted us to have a desire to imitate his sovereignty in this way. This desire in itself should not automatically be called "greed," because that word slanders something that is a good desire given to us by God.[29]

To summarize, *The Bible* demonstrates that God is the ultimate owner of all property and source of all private property rights or ownership in the temporal sense. Part of the God-given jurisdiction of the civil magistrate is to protect and enforce these God-given and God-instituted rights. Thus, the source of private property rights is God, and the justification for those property rights being protected by the civil government by their inclusion in the legal system is that God has, in His wisdom, included this as a part of the

[28] Rushdoony, *Institutes of Biblical Law* 450-451.

[29] Grudem, *Business for the Glory of God* 19-20 (emphasis in original).

jurisdiction of the civil government. The civil government does not create the right to own private property but rather enforces a right already granted by God.

II. The Creation of Private Property Rights

A natural question that arises when considering private property rights is how those rights are created or assigned. In other words, how does one come to own something? In order to think through this question, consider how James Kent, sometimes referred to as the American Blackstone,[30] answers it in his *Commentaries on American Law*. Then, consider the famous case of *Pierson v. Post* and compare the majority opinion with the dissent.

James Kent
2 Commentaries on American Law 318-320 (1824)

Having concluded a series of lectures on the various rights of persons, I proceed next to the examination of the law of property, which has always occupied a preeminent place in the municipal codes of every civilized people. I purpose to begin with the law of personal property, as it appears to be the most natural and easy transition from the subjects which we have already discussed. This is the species of property which first arises, and is cultivated in the rudest ages; and when commerce and the arts have ascended to distinguished heights, it maintains its level, if it does not rise even superior to property in land itself, in the influence which it exercises over the talents, the passions, and the destiny of mankind.

To suppose a state of man prior to the existence of any notions of separate property, when all things were common, and when men throughout the world lived, without law or government, in innocence and simplicity, is a mere dream of the imagination. It is the golden age of the poets which forms such a delightful picture in the fictions, adorned by the muse of Hesiod, Lucretius, Ovid, and Virgil. It has been truly observed that the first man who was born into the world killed the second; and when did the times of simplicity begin? And yet we find the Roman historians and philosophers rivaling the language of poetry in their descriptions of some imaginary state of nature, which it was impossible to know and idle to conjecture. No such state was intended for man in the benevolent dispensation of Providence; and in following the migrations of nations, apart from the book of Genesis, human curiosity is unable to penetrate beyond the pages of genuine history; and Homer, Herodotus, and Livy carry us back to the confines of the fabulous ages. The sense of property is inherent in the human breast, and the gradual enlargement and cultivation of that sense, from its feeble force in the savage

---

[30] William Blackstone is a famous commentator on the laws of England, and his work was very influential on both English and early American law.

state, to its full vigor and maturity among polished nations, forms a very instructive portion of the history of civil society. Man was fitted and intended by the Author of his being for society and government, and for the acquisition and enjoyment of property. It is, to speak correctly, the law of his nature; and by obedience to this law, he brings all his faculties into exercise, and is enabled ◁*A* to display the various and exalted powers of the human mind.

Occupancy, doubtless, gave the first title to property, in lands and movables. It is the natural and original method of acquiring it; and upon the principles of universal law, that the title continues so long as occupancy continues. There is no person, even in his rudest state, who does not feel and acknowledge, in a greater or less degree, the justice of this title. The right of property, founded on occupancy, is suggested to the human mind by feeling and reason prior to the influence of positive institutions. There have been modern theorists who have considered separate and exclusive property, and inequalities of property, as the cause of injustice, and the unhappy result of government and artificial institutions. But human society would be in a most unnatural and miserable condition if it were possible to be instituted or reorganized upon the basis of such speculations. The sense of property is graciously bestowed on mankind for the purpose of rousing them from sloth, and stimulating them to action; and so long as the right of acquisition is ◁*K* exercised in conformity to the social relations, and the moral obligations which spring from them, it ought to be sacredly protected. The natural and active sense of property pervades the foundations of social improvement. It leads to the cultivation of the earth, the institution of government, the establishment of justice, the acquisition of the comforts of life, the growth of the useful arts, the spirit of commerce, the productions of taste, the erections of charity, and the display of the benevolent affections.

Pierson v. Post
3 Caines 175, 2 A.D. 264 (N.Y. Sup. Ct. 1805)

---

* * *

TOMPKINS, J. delivered the opinion of the court.

This cause comes before us on a return to a *certiorari* directed to one of the justices of *Queens* county.

The question submitted by the counsel in this cause for our determination is, whether *Lodowick Post,* by the pursuit with his hounds in the manner alleged in his declaration, acquired such a right to, or property in, the fox, as will sustain an action against *Pierson* for killing and taking him away?

The cause was argued with much ability by the counsel on both sides, and presents for our decision a novel and nice question. It is admitted that a fox is an animal *feræ naturæ,* and that property in such animals is acquired by occupancy only.   These admissions narrow the discussion to the simple question of what acts amount to occupancy, applied to acquiring right to wild animals?

If we have recourse to the ancient writers upon general principles of law, the judgment below is obviously erroneous. *Justinian's Institutes,* lib. 2. tit. 1. s. 13. and *Fleta,* lib. 3. c. 2. p. 175. adopt the principle, that pursuit alone vests no property or right in the huntsman; and that even pursuit, accompanied with wounding, is equally ineffectual for that purpose, unless the animal be actually taken. The same principle is recognised by *Bracton,* lib. 2. c. 1. p. 8.

Puffendorf, lib. 4. c. 6. s. 2. and 10. defines occupancy of beasts *feræ naturæ,* to be the actual corporal possession of them, and *Bynkershoek* is cited as coinciding in this definition. It is indeed with hesitation that *Puffendorf* affirms that a wild beast mortally wounded, or greatly maimed, cannot be fairly intercepted by another, whilst the pursuit of the person inflicting the wound continues. The foregoing authorities are decisive to show that mere pursuit gave *Post* no legal right to the fox, but that he became the property of *Pierson,* who intercepted and killed him.

It therefore only remains to inquire whether there are any contrary principles, or authorities, to be found in other books, which ought to induce a different decision. Most of the cases which have occurred in *England,* relating to property in wild animals, have either been discussed and decided upon the principles of their positive statute regulations, or have arisen between the huntsman and the owner of the land upon which beasts *feræ naturæ* have been apprehended; the former claiming them by title of occupancy, and the latter *ratione soli.* Little satisfactory aid can, therefore, be derived from the *English* reporters.

Barbeyrac, in his notes on *Puffendorf,* does not accede to the definition of occupancy by the latter, but, on the contrary, affirms, that actual bodily seizure is not, in all cases, necessary to constitute possession of wild animals. He does not, however, *describe* the acts which, according to his ideas, will amount to an appropriation of such animals to private use, so as to exclude the claims of all other persons, by title of occupancy, to the same animals; and he is far from averring that pursuit alone is sufficient for that purpose. To a certain extent, and as far as *Barbeyrac* appears to me to go, his objections to *Puffendorf's* definition of occupancy are reasonable and correct. That is to say, that actual bodily seizure is not indispensable to acquire right to, or possession of, wild beasts; but that, on the contrary, the mortal wounding of such beasts, by one not abandoning his pursuit, may, with the utmost propriety, be deemed possession of him; since, thereby, the pursuer manifests an unequivocal intention of appropriating the animal to his individual use, has deprived him of his natural liberty, and brought him within his certain control. So also, encompassing and securing such animals with nets and toils, or otherwise intercepting them in such a manner as to deprive them of their natural liberty, and render escape impossible, may justly be deemed to give possession of them to those persons who, by their industry and labour, have used such means of apprehending them. *Barbeyrac* seems to have adopted, and had in view in his notes, the more accurate opinion of *Grotius,* with respect to occupancy. That celebrated author, lib. 2. c. 8. s. 3. p. 309. speaking of occupancy, proceeds thus: "*Requiritur autem corporalis quœdam possessio ad dominium adipiscendum; atque ideo, vulnerasse non sufficit.*" But in the following section he explains and qualifies this definition of occupancy: "*Sed possessio illa potest non solis manibus, sed instrumentis, ut decipulis, retibus, laqueis dum duo adsint: primum ut ipsa instrumenta sint in nostra potestate, deinde ut fera, ita inclusa sit, ut exire inde nequeat.*" This qualification embraces the full extent of *Barbeyrac's* objection to *Puffendorf's* definition, and allows as great a latitude to acquiring property by occupancy, as can reasonably be inferred from the words or ideas expressed by *Barbeyrac* in his notes. The case now under consideration is one of mere pursuit, and presents no circumstances or acts which can bring it within the definition of occupancy by *Puffendorf,* or *Grotius,* or the ideas of *Barbeyrac* upon that subject.

The case cited from 11 *Mod.* 74—130. I think clearly distinguishable from the present; inasmuch as there the action was for maliciously hindering and disturbing the plaintiff in the exercise and enjoyment of a private franchise; and in the report of the same case, 3 *Salk.* 9. *Holt,* Ch. J. states, that the ducks were in the plaintiff's decoy pond, and *so in his possession,* from which it is obvious the court laid much stress in their opinion upon the plaintiff's possession of the ducks, *ratione soli.*

We are the more readily inclined to confine possession or occupancy of beasts *ferœ naturœ,* within the limits prescribed by the learned authors above cited, for the sake of certainty, and preserving peace and order in society. If the first seeing, starting, or pursuing such animals, without having so wounded, circumvented or ensnared them, so as to deprive them of their natural liberty, and subject them to the control of their pursuer, should afford the basis of actions against others for intercepting and killing them, it would prove a fertile source of quarrels and litigation.

However uncourteous or unkind the conduct of *Pierson* towards *Post,* in this instance, may have been, yet his act was productive of no injury or damage for which a legal remedy can be applied. We are of opinion the judgment below was erroneous, and ought to be reversed.

LIVINGSTON, J. My opinion differs from that of the court.

Of six exceptions, taken to the proceedings below, all are abandoned except the third, which reduces the controversy to a single question.

Whether a person who, with his own hounds, starts and hunts a fox on waste and uninhabited ground, and is on the point of seizing his prey, acquires such an interest in the animal, as to have a right of action against another, who in view of the huntsman and his dogs in full pursuit, and with knowledge of the chase, shall kill and carry him away?

This is a knotty point, and should have been submitted to the arbitration of sportsmen, without poring over *Justinian, Fleta, Bracton, Puffendorf, Locke, Barbeyrac,* or *Blackstone,* all of whom have been cited; they would have had no difficulty in coming to a prompt and correct conclusion. In a court thus constituted, the skin and carcass of poor *reynard* would have been properly disposed of, and a precedent set, interfering with no usage or custom which the experience of ages has sanctioned, and which must be so well known to every votary of *Diana.* But the parties have referred the question to our judgment, and we must dispose of it as well as we can, from the partial lights we possess, leaving to a higher tribunal, the correction of any mistake which we may be so unfortunate as to make. By the pleadings it is admitted that a fox is a "wild and noxious beast." Both parties have regarded him, as the law of nations does a pirate, *"hostem humani generis,"* and although *"de mortuis nil nisi bonum,"* be a maxim of our profession, the memory of the deceased has not been spared. His depredations on farmers and on barn yards, have not been forgotten; and to put him to death wherever found, is allowed to be meritorious, and of public benefit. Hence it follows, that our decision should have in view the greatest possible encouragement to the destruction of an animal, so cunning and ruthless in his career. But who would keep a pack of hounds; or what gentleman, at the sound of the horn, and at peep of day, would mount his steed, and for hours together, *"sub jove frigido,"* or a vertical sun, pursue the windings of this wily quadruped, if, just as night came on, and his stratagems and strength were nearly exhausted, a saucy intruder, who had not shared in the honours or labours of the chase, were permitted to come in at the death, and bear away in triumph the object of pursuit? Whatever *Justinian* may have thought of the matter, it must be recollected that his code was compiled many hundred years ago, and it would be very hard indeed, at the distance of so many centuries, not to have a right to establish a rule for ourselves. In his day, we read of no order of men who made it a business, in the language of the declaration in this cause, "with hounds and dogs to find, start, pursue, hunt, and chase," these animals, and that, too, without any other motive than the preservation of *Roman* poultry; if this diversion had been then in fashion, the lawyers who composed his institutes, would have taken care not to pass it by, without suitable encouragement. If any thing, therefore, in the digests or pandects shall appear to militate against the defendant in error, who, on this occasion, was the foxhunter, we have only to say *tempora mutantur;* and if men themselves change with the times, why should not laws also undergo an alteration?

It may be expected, however, by the learned counsel, that more particular notice be taken of their authorities. I have examined them all, and feel great difficulty in determining, whether to acquire dominion over a thing, before in common, it be sufficient that we barely see it, or know where it is, or wish for it, or make a declaration of our will respecting it; or whether, in the case of wild beasts, setting a trap, or lying in wait, or starting, or pursuing, be enough; or if an actual wounding, or killing, or bodily tact and occupation be necessary.   Writers on general law, who have favoured us with their speculations on these points, differ on them all; but, great as is the diversity of sentiment among them, some conclusion must be adopted on the question immediately before us. After mature deliberation, I embrace that of *Barbeyrac*, as the most rational, and least liable to objection. If at liberty, we might imitate the courtesy of a certain emperor, who, to avoid giving offence to the advocates of any of these different doctrines, adopted a middle course, and by ingenious distinctions, rendered it difficult to say (as often happens after a fierce and angry contest) to whom the palm of victory belonged. He ordained, that if a beast be followed with *large dogs and hounds,* he shall belong to the hunter, not to the chance occupant; and in like manner, if he be killed or wounded with a lance or sword; but if chased with *beagles only,* then he passed to the captor, not to the first pursuer. If slain with a dart, a sling, or a bow, he fell to the hunter, if still in chase, and not to him who might afterwards find and seize him.

Now, as we are without any municipal regulations of our own, and the pursuit here, for aught that appears on the case, being with dogs and hounds of *imperial stature,* we are at liberty to adopt one of the provisions just cited, which comports also with the learned conclusion of *Barbeyrac,* that property in animals *feræ naturæ* may be acquired without bodily touch or manucaption, provided the pursuer be within reach, or have a *reasonable* prospect (which certainly existed here) of taking, what he has *thus* discovered an intention of converting to his own use.

When we reflect also that the interest of our husbandmen, the most useful of men in any community, will be advanced by the destruction of a beast so pernicious and incorrigible, we cannot greatly err, in saying, that a pursuit like the present, through waste and unoccupied lands, and which must inevitably and speedily have terminated in corporal possession, or bodily *seisin,* confers such a right to the object of it, as to make any one a wrongdoer, who shall interfere and shoulder the spoil. The *justice's* judgment ought, therefore, in my opinion, to be affirmed.

Notes and Questions

---

1. Reasoning from Generals to Particulars.   The issue of the relationship of generals to particulars has plagued philosophers for millennia. It is at least as old as Plato and Aristotle. In fact, the famous painting by the Italian Renaissance artist Raphael, called the *School of Athens,* is meant to capture this debate. Plato in the fresco is pointing up, in reference to the general principles (or forms as Plato understood them) being the most important thing, while Aristotle is portrayed with his hand down, indicating that reality actually resides most ultimately in the various particulars.

Despite the many attempts at resolution throughout the years by philosophers holding various worldviews, it is only within a Christian worldview that this issue can be satisfactorily resolved. In fact, only within a Christian worldview do we have any reason to believe that there would be any relationship between the generals and particulars at all.[31]

In a naturalistic evolutionary worldview, such as the one underpinning law and economics, where everything is simply governed by time and chance operating upon matter (and chaos is therefore king), why would one expect there to be any relationship between generals and particulars? Why would one expect to see order? Why would one have reason to believe that what has happened in the past is in any way indicative of what will happen in the future?

Indeed, many non-Christian thinkers have come to this conclusion. Generally, they have decided to live as if what their philosophies or worldviews teach is not true and assume that there is, in fact, a reason to expect order in the world. They have generally sought a connection between generals and particulars, even though their worldviews tell them there should be none.

In the Christian worldview, we have every reason to believe that generals and particulars relate because a sovereign and loving Lord created the universe and sustains it still. *See Colossians* 1:17 and *Hebrews* 1:3 (Christ is even now "upholding all things by the word of his power"). Therefore, the order in the universe comes from the Creator. We should expect to be able to discover this order and guiding principles within this order (generals or universals) and then be able to rationally apply these generals to various situations (particulars.)

Let's take an example from the Scriptures. In answering a question posed to Him, Jesus said, in *Matthew* 22:37-40, that:

> Thou shalt love the Lord thy God with all thy heart, and with all thy soul, and with all thy mind. This is the first and great commandment. And the second is like unto it, Thou shalt love thy neighbour as thyself. On these two commandments hang all the law and the prophets.

It is important to note that Jesus does not stop with the statement of the two greatest commandments (presumably therefore the two greatest general principles), but He goes on to assert that on these two commandments all of the rest of Scripture hangs.

Thus, upon hearing that "love God" is the greatest commandment, one might ask, "how do I love God?" Without Jesus' second assertion, this might be very difficult to answer. But, by applying Jesus' words, it becomes much easier to answer. Why? Because *The Bible* gives us not only general principles but more particular applications of those principles as well. Accordingly, as we look into *The Bible* to find how we should love God, we find that one way to love Him is to have no other gods before Him. Another way is to make no

---

[31] Or, for that matter, between the particulars themselves. The particulars could just be random, unconnected, chaotic events. In fact, it would be fair to ask, from an evolutionary point of view, why one would expect to see any order or meaning in the world at all.

graven images or idols. In addition, one loves God by not taking His name in vain. God is also loved when we honor the Sabbath day and keep it holy. *See Exodus* 20:1-8; *Deuteronomy* 6:5 and 5:6-12.

You have probably already noticed that the above list contains the first four of the Ten Commandments, which are often referred to as the first table of the law. We can do the same thing with the last six of the Ten Commandments, or the second table of the law.

How do I love my neighbor as myself? One way is to honor my father and mother. Other ways include not committing murder, adultery, or theft. Also, if I want to love my neighbor, I should not bear false witness against him nor covet anything that God has entrusted to him. *See Leviticus* 19:18; *Exodus* 20:9-17; and *Deuteronomy* 5:13-21.

As you can see, we are moving from broad general principles (i.e., love God) to more specific application of those principles (i.e., don't commit adultery.) And, of course, we need not stop there. There are increasing levels of specificity contained within the Scriptures. For instance, one might inquire as to the meaning of "do not commit adultery." Is that limited only to sexual intercourse with someone to whom one is not married?

In the Sermon on the Mount, Jesus answers this question in the negative. He asserts that the actual general rule is much broader than that. He states that "do not commit adultery" includes also not lusting after a woman in your heart. Thus, we might state this process of moving from generality to increasing particularity in this way: one of the ways in which one should love his neighbor is by exercising and demonstrating sexual purity. Sexual purity includes not committing the physical act of adultery, but it also goes much further, even to the point of including the specific command that one should not even lust after his neighbor's wife.[32]

Reasoning from generality to specificity, as we have been doing above, is a biblical way of thinking, and it only makes sense in a Christian worldview where order can be expected in the world. As noted earlier, because God is the Creator and Sustainer of the world, we can expect to find order and relationship in the world. Thus, reasoning from generality to particularity is possible. The humanistic, naturalistic, evolutionary worldview that underpins the economic analysis of law cannot hope to provide this type of framework to support reasoning from generals to particulars in this way.

Not surprisingly, law and economics scholars, and the American Legal Realists from which they descend, tend to reject this type of thinking. Demonstrating his rejection of the highest of generals, a law above the law or the law of nature and nature's God as a source of law, Oliver Wendell Holmes famously wrote in a dissenting opinion in *Southern Pacific Company v. Jensen*, 244 U.S. 205, 222 (1917) that "[t]he common law is not a brooding omnipresence in the sky, but the articulate voice of some sovereign or quasi

---

[32] Note that by not lusting after other women, a man is also loving his wife (or future wife, as the case may be.) Obviously, the reverse could be stated from the female perspective and it would be equally valid.

sovereign that can be identified." Further, it is often asserted by legal skeptics that one can take any set of facts and then apply the law to it and reach any outcome, thereby asserting that reasoning from general principles to specific situations is inherently manipuable and not subject to accurate conclusions. However, this type of argumentation is what lawyers do all the time! Thus, as Professor Steven D. Smith aptly points out, this gives the law a feeling of being nothing more than a great charade or performance with nothing but policy considerations going on underneath. He also aptly points out that the assertion that this has been what has been transpiring for centuries in the law is highly unlikely. Rather, law and economics scholars, like Judge Posner, actually have a reformist goal—in other words they think law *should* be done this way.[33]

Despite the arguments of law and economics scholars and the American Legal Realists before them that reasoning from generals to particulars should be abandoned for mere policy analysis, the issue of the discerning of generals or universals and their relationship and application to particulars is foundational to the practice of law. Certainly historically, and even still today, in the Western legal tradition, much of the work of law consists of identifying general rules and principles and applying those generals to various specific situations.

Virtually every area of law contains general rules that are applied to specific cases by judges and juries.[34] To help illustrate this, let's consider a general rule from property law, which was at issue in *Pierson*.

Kent sets out the general rule that a property right is only gained by occupancy or dominion. In *Pierson*, the question is how does one gain occupancy or dominion over a wild animal such that a property right in the animal arises. Is mere pursuit enough, or does it require actual physical possession? Or is it something else?

Looking at this general rule, what do you think? Who applied the rule most correctly and faithfully in *Pierson*, the majority or the dissent? Who seems to be most concerned about actually deciding what the accurate rule is and how it should be applied, the majority or the dissent?

2. *Judicial v. Prudential Reasoning.* In the previous note, we saw that the relationship of generals to particulars is foundational to American law, and that this foundational idea only makes sense in a Christian worldview. In this note, we will consider another foundational idea in American law: the contrast between judicial and prudential reasoning. Like the issue of general and particulars, the concept of judicial v. prudential

---

[33] Smith, *Law's Quandary* 78-81.

[34] Does this also apply to legislatures such as the United States Congress? Unfortunately, we do not often think of it in quite this way, but we should. Congress should be attempting to pass specific pieces of legislation (particulars) that are in accord with the principles upon which God has built the world. For example, in earlier eras, if a bill was proposed in Congress, the proponent of the bill might expect to be asked where he found support for such an idea in *The Bible*. Regrettably, such a discussion is unimaginable today.

reasoning also impacts the law in a variety of ways. And, like the issue of general and particulars, the concept of judicial v. prudential reasoning presents a stark contrast between the Christian view of law and the law and economics approach.

The American constitutional system includes as one of its core principles the idea that liberty is best ensured in a system that includes a robust separation of powers. Separation of powers is simply the idea that the powers of government should be separated into various departments or institutions. In our system, this includes a separation between the judicial branch and the legislative branch.

This idea is based upon a solid biblical foundation. While the prevailing secular humanist worldview understands man to be essentially good and perfectable, the biblical worldview understands man's fallen condition. Fallen men are prone to selfishness and evil, and we all struggle to act altruistically. To paraphrase the *Federalist Papers*, men are not angels. *See, e.g., Genesis* 3 and *Romans* 3:9-23.

Since men are not angels, a separation of powers works to limit the consolidation of power in any one person or institution. By limiting the power any one person or institution can wield, freedom is better preserved.

Most Americans wholeheartedly support the idea of a separation of powers within our system. Generally, we, as a people, are very proud of our Constitutional system and its features. However, unfortunately, our understanding of what these principles actually mean has greatly diminished, even among those who should know better.

One such striking example related to this issue is the difference between political and judicial powers, roles, and decision-making. Judges and the courts are entrusted with judicial power and should engage in judicial reasoning, while the legislature is entrusted with legislative power and should engage in legislative reasoning. Jeffrey S. Tuomala,[35] in his excellent article entitled *Marbury v. Madison and the Foundation of Law,* describes these two types of power and their correlative styles of reasoning as follows:

> The action of legislating, which includes the adoption of a constitution, is forward-looking or prospective in nature. The focus in the legislative process is not upon determining what happened at some particular time in the past in some discrete situation. The focus is on formulating rules best designed to achieve some lawful object of government. The process of legislation may entail codifying preexisting law, be it inalienable rights or general principles of law, but its distinguishing characteristic is that it designs positive enactments to best achieve legitimate government objectives. The second characteristic that distinguishes the legislative

---

[35] Dean Tuomala is a faculty member at Liberty University School of Law. He was the Law School's founding Associate Dean for Academic Affairs.

from the judicial process is that legislation is framed in general terms regulating all persons similarly situated.

The process of adjudication, on the other hand, has a focus that is backward-looking in nature. Adjudication is designed to determine what happened to a relatively limited number of persons at some discrete time in the past. A court applies already existing law, be it acts of Congress, general principles of law, or the Constitution, to the facts of a case in order to determine whether a legal duty has been breached. If it has been, the court applies a remedy focused on restoring the victim, not achieving some future objective. Adjudication applies with particularity to a limited number of persons who are parties to a lawsuit.

The exercise of the executive power, which like the exercise of the legislative power is forward-looking in nature, is designed to best achieve the legislative objects. The executive and legislative powers, as well as the power of appointment, are political or prudential in nature. . . .

Congress, in exercising the legislative power, makes judgments as to the best means of achieving constitutional objectives or ends. The President makes his best judgment in allocating resources and applying force to achieve those ends. . . . The judicial power does not entail the exercise of will (courts do not make law; the law already exists), and it does not entail the use of force (courts do not execute their own judgments; they depend upon the executive branch). Courts exercise only judgment—not political judgment that is forward-looking, but judicial judgment that is backward-looking in nature.[36]

A little later in his article, Dean Tuomala makes clear that the difference between judicial power (and reasoning) and legislative power (and prudential reasoning) is found, not only in the Declaration of Independence, but also in the Scriptures and the person of God Himself. He writes:

Just as the doctrines of judicial review and general principles of law are grounded in the jurisprudence of the Declaration of Independence, so also is the doctrine distinguishing between the judicial and political powers. Civil officers exercise those powers in a manner that is reflective and imitative of the manner in which God governs the affairs of

---

[36] Jeffrey C. Tuomala, *Marbury v. Madison and the Foundation of Law*, 4 Liberty U.L. Rev. 297, 329-330 (2010). As noted at the end of chapter 1, I would highly recommend that you read this important article by Dean Tuomala in its entirety. It is absolutely essential to understanding law and the American system.

men and nations—as "Supreme Judge of the World" and as "Divine Providence." The exercise of judicial power as an application of established law to past conduct is demonstrated through the operation of the office of Supreme Judge of the World.   In fact, the Declaration comprises the essential elements of a legal complaint—a statement of the judge's jurisdiction to hear the case ("Supreme Judge" with universal jurisdiction), a cause of action ("long train of abuses" that violated "unalienable rights"), and a remedy (independence/separation from England).

God also directs and governs, by His will and His law, that which He has created. The reference to God as "Divine Providence" describes Him in that office as the One who sees the end from the beginning and governs all things toward their appointed ends.   The signers of the Declaration of Independence, convinced of the rightness of their cause and bound to one another by oath, moved forward with a firm reliance on God's protection. The nature of political powers as forward-looking and directed to enumerated ends is demonstrated through the operation of the office of Divine Providence.[37]

In *Pierson*, did the majority opinion engage in judicial or prudential reasoning? What about the dissent? Does one opinion appear to follow a law and economics approach more than the other? How can you tell?

---

[37] *Id.* at 331-333 (citing, among other authorities, Revelation 20:11-13; Romans 3:25-26 and 8:1-4; Isaiah 53:5 and 2:1-6; Ephesians 1:11; Colossians 1:17; and 1 Peter 1:18-19.)

I. Definition of a Contract and Jurisdiction of the Civil Magistrate to Enforce Promises

A logical place to begin your study of contract law would be by asking the simple question, "What is a contract?" A simple and straightforward definition for a contract is a promise or a set of promises that the civil magistrate will enforce with legal sanctions. Obviously, not all promises are enforceable by the civil magistrate. To state this important point another way, not all promises are within the jurisdiction of the civil government. In other words, not all promises give rise to contracts.

Of course, the preceding implies that there is a proper role, or sphere of action, or jurisdiction, within which the civil government should operate. And, indeed, *The Bible* does appear to provide for four different types of "government"—self-government, family government, church government, and civil government, each with its own sphere of action or jurisdiction.[38] While there is some overlap in the jurisdictions, and some gray areas, each type of government has a God-ordained set of duties and responsibilities. No human institution or government has unlimited jurisdiction—only Jesus Christ, the King of kings and Lord of lords enjoys unlimited, universal jurisdiction. Accordingly, as the Founding Fathers and many others throughout history have understood, it is important for human institutions to be limited in their jurisdictional reach if liberty is to be secured and a free society fostered.

While it is far beyond the scope of this work to consider the proper jurisdiction of each of the four forms of government found in *The Bible*, it is useful and necessary for our work in this course to at least consider the proper jurisdiction of the civil magistrate. Writing of the proper role of the civil magistrate in his excellent article *A Biblical Model for Analysis of Issues of Law and Public Policy: with Illustrative Applications to Contracts, Antitrust,*

---

[38] *See, e.g.,* Galatians 5:22-23, Colossians 3:18-21, Ephesians 5:24-6:4, Hebrews 13:17, 1 Timothy 3:1-13, Romans 13:1-7; 1 Peter 2:13-17; Roger Bern, *A Biblical Model for Analysis of Issues of Law and Public Policy: with Illustrative Applications to Contracts, Antitrust, Remedies and Public Policy Issues,* 6 Regent U. L. Rev. 103, 116-131 (1995), Herbert W. Titus, *God, Man, and Law: The Biblical Principles* 64-97 (1994), and David W. Hall, *Savior or Servant? Putting Government in its Place* (1996).

Remedies and Public Policy Issues, the late Professor Roger Bern[39] summarizes the role of the civil magistrate in the following:

(9) Neither the Individual, nor any institution which God has established, has jurisdiction over all things, but each has been granted limited jurisdiction in which to function.

(10) The principle of limited jurisdiction for Civil Government was confirmed by Jesus when He stated, "render to Caesar the things that are Caesar's, and to God the things that are God's." Caesar is not given control over all things.

(11) The jurisdiction of Civil Government exists in relationship to, and is best described and understood in terms of, duties owed to God by the Individual, the Family and the Church.

(12) All sin is lawlessness, and all who sin are answerable to God because He has jurisdiction over all things, even the heart of man. But not all sin is within the jurisdiction of Civil Government, which has jurisdiction with respect to wrongful conduct by man, but not with respect to wrongful thoughts or heart motives.

(13) Civil Government is God's avenger on earth, with jurisdiction to punish evildoers (those who do *kakos*), prevent threatened harm, provide redress for harm caused, and to commend those who do well.

(14) Included within the category of "evildoer" is one who does an act which is innately evil, whether it causes harm to another or not, and also one who interferes with another's carrying out his duties to God. With respect to both types of actions, Civil Government has a duty to be God's avenger, bringing to bear the coercive sanction appropriate to the action.

(15) When Civil Government punishes evildoers, prevents threatened evildoing, provides for redress for harm caused, and commends those who do well, it fulfills its duties to God and concomitantly contributes to or facilitates an environment in which the Individual, the Family and the Church may fulfill their respective duties to God in all godliness and dignity.

---

[39] I had the pleasure of getting to know, learning from, and working with Professor Bern at Liberty University School of Law. I started teaching at the Law School as an adjunct in the spring of 2006, and I joined the full-time faculty in January of 2007. Professor Bern was truly a pioneer and leader in Christian legal education, and I am very thankful that God gave me the opportunity to cross paths with this great man. He passed away on November 26, 2007, and he is still sorely missed. I would highly recommend to you his *Biblical Model* article and any and all of his other works.

(16) Civil Government does not have jurisdiction to compel general love or affirmative expressions of love by an individual or group toward others.[40]

Further, in the section of his article that applies the Biblical Model to the contracts setting in particular, Professor Bern states:

> One of the ways man may more effectively carry out his stewardship-dominion duties[41] to God is by entering into agreements with his fellows. Such agreements are possible because, in creating man in His own image, God has endowed man with language, the ability to communicate with words. In particular, He has given man the ability to communicate with words of a special quality—words of promise. The essence of such words, spoken by one created in the image of God, is to instill in the one who hears them a confidence, an expectation, that they will be kept.[42]

Thus, God has given humans the ability to make promises and bind themselves by their words. Some promises are of such a character that, if they are not kept, the breaking rises to the level of evil-doing or *kakos*,[43] such that the civil magistrate should intervene with legal sanctions. Other promises do not rise to such a level, and they are therefore outside of the jurisdiction of the civil magistrate.

In order to illustrate, an example might be helpful. If I promise my wife that I will mow the yard on Thursday evenings after work, there is a sense in which I have broken my word and therefore acted unethically or immorally if I fail to do so. However, my wife will not be able to go to the Bedford Circuit

---

[40] Bern, *Biblical Model* at 122-25 (citations omitted).

[41] In line with other Christian thinkers in the Western legal tradition, Prof. Bern asserts that our rights derive from the duties that we owe to God. For example, we have a duty to God to be chaste and sexually pure, and we have a right that others not interfere with our fulfillment of this duty to God. Another example would be our duty to worship God, which gives rise to a corresponding right that others not interfere with our worship of God. Johannes Althusius, for example, understood rights this way. *See, e.g., Natural Rights, Popular Sovereignty, and Covenant Politics: Johannes Althusius and the Dutch Revolt and Republic* in John Witte, Jr., *The Reformation of Rights: Law, Religion, and Human Rights in Early Modern Calvinism* 143-207 (2007).

In the context of the Prof. Bern quotation above, the stewardship-dominion duties are derived from God's initial command to Adam and Eve to take dominion over the Earth in *Genesis* 1:28-29 and His reiteration of that command to Noah after the flood in *Genesis* 9:1-7. Prof. Bern states this important duty this way: "man has a duty to God to govern his own life and to steward all that he is and has in a way that glorifies God." Bern, *Biblical Model* at 119 n.84. This duty is particularly important when considering contracts, property rights, and other commercial or business areas of law.

[42] Bern, *Biblical Model* at 131-132 (citations omitted).

[43] *Kakos* is the Greek word used in both Romans 13:4 (translated in the King James Version as "him that doeth evil") and 1 Peter 2:14 (translated in the King James Version as "evildoers").

Court in Virginia, where we live, and sue me for breach of contract. In this example, I have acted unethically or immorally but not "illegally." My promise to mow on Thursday evenings was not a contract. The civil magistrate will not sanction me for failing to fulfill this promise. (Although, for repeated offenses of this nature, there may well be sanctions within the jurisdiction of family government and perhaps even church government in more serious situations. Certainly, failing to mow the yard persistently will have undesirable consequences such as the kids not being able to play in the yard due to the tall grass, ticks, etc., and it will look terrible, which would not be loving my neighbors.) To put it another way, this promise is outside the jurisdiction of the civil magistrate.

By contrast, if I promise to sell my neighbor five laying hens for ten dollars each, and I break that promise, he can sue me for breach of that promise. It is a contract, and it is enforceable by the civil magistrate with legal sanctions because it is within the jurisdiction of the civil magistrate.

Accordingly, you can see that, for a proper understanding of contracts law, it is very important to be able to determine which promises are actually contracts, i.e., within the jurisdiction of the civil magistrate, and which are not. Determining this will in turn determine whether or not the civil magistrate can be called upon to enforce the promise or set of promises with legal sanctions. This leads naturally to the requirements, or elements, for a valid, enforceable contract. These elements are agreement (which includes offer and acceptance), consideration, contractual capacity, and legality.

The following case presents an interesting illustration of these issues. As you read it consider: (1) whether the elements of a valid, enforceable contract exist under these facts, (2) whether some other theory should be used for the civil magistrate to enforce this promise even if the elements of a valid, enforceable contract are not satisfied, and (3) whether this is the type of promise that should be within the jurisdiction of the civil magistrate or the family or perhaps both.

Calabro v. Calabro
15 S.W.3d 873 (Tenn. Ct. App. 1999)

This appeal involves a suit for breach of contract. Plaintiff, Belinda Hope Calabro, appeals from the order of the trial court granting summary judgement to defendant, Arthur Donald Calabro.

Plaintiff, Hope Calabro, is the daughter of the defendant, Arthur Calabro. Arthur Calabro and Hope's mother were divorced when Hope was four years old. From the time of the divorce until Hope Calabro finished high school she lived in Oklahoma with her mother who was granted sole custody of Hope at the time of the divorce procedings [*sic*]. During all times material to this case defendant lived in Memphis, Tennessee. He provided financial support to Hope while she was living with her mother including an allowance, an automobile, and travel expenses. While Hope Calabro was growing up, Arthur Calabro saw her during summers and on some holidays.

Hope Calabro had an excellent [sic] academic record in high school. During her senior year of high school Arthur Calabro offered to pay his daughter's expenses to attend a distinguished, private universisty [sic] if she received at least $10,000.00 in financial aid. At the time that Hope Calabro was applying to colleges, she knew that she was eligible to attend the University of Oklahoma and receive a full scholarship, sufficient to pay tuition, room, board, books, and student activity fee. Knowing that her father would be willing to finance her college education at a private college if she received $10,000.00 in financial aid, Hope applied to and was accepted at Boston University, Tulane University, Pepperdine University, Stanford University, the University of California at San Diego, Southern Methodist University, and Vanderbilt University. Several of these schools offered her financial aid.

It is undisputed that in the fall of 1991 Hope Calabro enrolled in and began attending Vanderbilt University with her father paying expenses that exceeded her scholarship. It is also undisputed that during the Christmas break of 1992 Arthur Calabro informed Hope Calabro that he was no longer willing to pay for her college expenses. Both parties agree that at that time he had prepaid her tuition for the spring of 1993 at Vanderbilt. It is undisputed that Plaintiff continued to attend Vanderbilt and completed her course work in the spring of 1995, earning a B.A. in psychology. What remains in dispute is whether Arthur Calabro formed a legally binding contract with his daughter to pay her college expenses and breached that contract by refusing to continue his support in December of 1992.

Plaintiff's complaint alleges that she moved to Nashville to attend Vanderbilt based upon defendant's representation that he would pay for all college tuition costs and living expenses in excess of plaintiff's scholarship while she was attending Vanderbilt. She avers that the defendant willfully repudiated his contract to pay all college tuition costs in excess of the scholarship that the plaintiff received, as well as all living expenses while she was attending Vanderbilt University. Plaintiff further alleges that due to his repudiation of the contract she financed these cost by taking out student loans that became due upon her graduation. Plaintiff demands compensatory damages representing the full extent of all college costs, including, but not limited to, outstanding student loans, personal living expenses during college, and other related expenses.

Defendant's answer admits that plaintiff attended Vanderbilt but denies that he made the representations as alleged in the complaint. Defendant admits that "he advised his daughter that if she entered and successfully remained in a course of study for the purpose of gaining admission to medical school, he would pay certain of her college related expenses while attending Vanderbilt University." He denies that plaintiff moved to Nashville and enrolled in Vanderbilt in response to his representation but admits that plaintiff enrolled in Vanderbilt and that she took out various student loans. He denies that he willfully repudiated his contract as alleged.

The trial court granted defendant summary judgment, and plaintiff has appealed, presenting three issues for review: (1) whether the trial court erred in holding that there was no valid consideration to support the defendant's promise of his offer to pay for his daughter's college expenses, (2) whether the court erred in holding that the contract between the parties was barred by the Statute of Frauds, and (3) whether the court erred in failing to enforce the defendant's promise under the doctrine of promissory estoppel. The trial court's order granting summary judgment did not state the reason therefor, and there is no transcript of the hearing on the motion for summary judgment to indicate that the trial judge made any such ruling from the bench. We perceive the dispositive issue to be whether the trial court erred in granting defendant's motion for summary judgment and will consider the arguments of counsel encompassed in the above-stated three issues.

A motion for summary judgment should be granted when the movant demonstrates that there are no genuine issues of material fact and that the moving party is entitled to a judgment as a matter of law. The party moving for summary judgment bears the burden of demonstrating that no genuine issue of material fact exists. On a motion for summary judgment, the court must take the strongest legitimate view of the evidence in favor of the nonmoving party, allow all reasonable inferences in favor of that party, and discard all countervailing evidence. . . .

Summary judgment is only appropriate when the facts and the legal conclusions drawn from the facts reasonably permit only one conclusion. If the facts are uncontroverted, summary judgment is inappropriate if reasonable minds could differ as to the inferences to be drawn therefrom. Since only questions of law are involved, there is no presumption of correctness regarding a trial court's grant of summary judgment. Therefore, our review of the trial court's grant of summary judgment is *de novo* on the record before this Court.

Plaintiff contends that there was a binding contract between the parties and that defendant breached the contract when he refused to continue paying for her college expenses. Plaintiff contends that she undertook to do something that she was not legally obligated to do, thereby providing the consideration needed to form a contract. She asserts that defendant received a benefit by having his daughter close to him and away from her mother's influence, and by having a well-educated daughter. Plaintiff further asserts that she gave up substantial scholarships and financial aid at the University of Oklahoma, Tulane, Southern Methodist University, and Pepperdine to attend Vanderbilt. Plaintiff asserts that these foregone opportunities, along with the substantial expense she incurred to attend Vanderbilt, constitute a legal detriment to her as promisee and consideration for her father's promise to pay her education expenses.

Plaintiff asserts that the Statute of Frauds presents no bar to the enforcement of defendant's oral promise to pay his daughter's college expenses. Plaintiff contends that at the very least she partially performed the contract and thus comes within the exception of the Statute of Frauds. She asserts that actually she has fully performed the unilateral contract by attending and graduating from Vanderbilt University. Furthermore plaintiff contends that the doctrine of promissory estoppel takes the contract out of the Statute of Frauds because she detrimentally relied on her father's promise.

Defendant contends that the trial court properly determined that he was entitled to summary judgment as to his daughter's claim relating to expenses and debt incurred after May 1993 because there is no genuine issue of any material fact. He asserts that as a parent he has no legal obligation to pay for the educational expenses of a child that has reached the age of majority. Arthur Calabro asserts that he did not intend to enter into a contract that legally obligated him to pay for college expenses, but merely desired to help his daughter realize the dream she expressed to him of becoming a doctor. He further contends that even if his generosity could be construed as an obligation, it is a moral rather than a legal obligation, which is not legally enforceable. He asserts that his daughter's college attendance was not a benefit to him and that his satisfaction at having Hope attend school near his home was not an inducement, because he made no such requirement. Defendant maintains that the cause of any detriment to Hope was her failure to excel in school, and he, in fact, suffered the detriment of the expense of two years of his daughter's education.

Finally defendant asserts that in December of 1992, he made it clear to his daughter that he would pay no more after May, 1993, and it was not reasonable, necessary or justifiable for Hope to return to Vanderbilt and rely on further financial support based on his gratuitous promise.

"A contract has been defined over the years as an agreement, upon sufficient consideration, to do or not to do a particular thing." A party attempting to prove the existence of a contract "is required to show that the agreement on which he relies was supported by adequate consideration . . ." "[I]n all simple contracts . . . whether written or verbal, the consideration must be averred and proved."

The question of what constitutes consideration adequate or sufficient to support a contract has been addressed by a number of Tennessee courts. The court in *University of Chattanooga v. Stansberry,* 9 Tenn.App. 341, 343 (1928) defined consideration as "either a benefit to the maker of the promise or a detriment to, or obligation upon the promisee." (*citing Foust v. Board of Education,* 76 Tenn., (8 Lea), 552). Courts have been willing to find a contract based on facts from which a jury could infer the requisite consideration.

> For there to be a consideration in a contract between parties to the contract it is not necessary that something concrete and tangible move from one to the other. Any benefit to one and detriment to the other may be a sufficient consideration. The jury may draw any reasonable and natural inference from the proof and if by inference from the proof a benefit to the promisor and detriment to the promisee might be inferred this will constitute a valid consideration.

Palmer v. Dehn, 29 Tenn.App. 597, 599, 198 S.W.2d 827, 828 (1946) . . .

. . .

Simply stated, plaintiff's evidence from her deposition testimony, and the deposition of Mr. Calabro's sister[44], is that Mr. Calabro promised to pay her tuition and expenses over and above the $10,000.00 scholarship if she attended Vanderbilt.   Plaintiff had previously been entitled to various scholarship opportunities at other colleges, but she relinquished those opportunities based upon the strength of defendant's promise. Although she preferred to go to another college, she deferred to Mr. Calabro's preference that she attend Vanderbilt. There was no condition attached to the promise to pay tuition that she maintain any sort of grade-point average or class standing, nor that she pursue any particular curriculum.

Defendant's testimony by deposition indicates that he did agree to pay the tuition and other expenses, but that he did not require that his daughter attend Vanderbilt. He admits that there was no condition attached that she pursue a pre-med curriculum or maintain a certain grade-point average.

We believe under the proof in this case that there is sufficient evidence to create a genuine issue of material fact as to whether there was adequate consideration flowing between the parties to constitute an enforceable contract. There is a dispute as to whether a benefit was conferred on defendant on his promise to pay the tuition and whether plaintiff suffered a detriment in her performance of the contract or agreement.

Defendant asserts that even if there was adequate consideration, the oral contract would be barred by the Statute of Frauds, T.C.A. § 29–2–101(a)(5)(1998), which provides:

> [U]pon any agreement or contract which is not to be performed within the space of one (1) year from the making of the agreement or contact; unless the promise or agreement, upon which such action shall be brought, or some memorandum or note thereof, shall be in writing, and signed by the party to be charged therewith, or some other person lawfully authorized by such party.

Plaintiff relies on her performance of the contract as excepting the contract from the operation of the statute.

The doctrine of part performance was utilized by the court in *Blasingame v. American Materials, Inc.,* 654 S.W.2d 659 (Tenn.1983) in enforcing an oral contract where over a period of years, the

---

[44] Mr. Calabro's sister testified that Mr. Calabro desired that his daughter attend Vanderbilt in order to be away from the influence of her mother and to be closer to him and thus strengthen the ties between father and daughter.

plaintiff was led to believe that the oral employment contract he made with defendant corporation would be honored; that in reliance thereon, plaintiff proceeded to perform his part of the bargain; and that in doing so, he so altered his position as to suffer an unconscionable loss if the corporation was allowed to rely on the Statue of Frauds. There is material evidence in this record to support those concurrent factual findings and they are binding on this Court.

Id. at 663. The Supreme Court found that such facts brought the plaintiff within the exception of part performance, and the plaintiff thereby avoided the Statute of Frauds. *Id.*

. . .

Plaintiff also relies upon the doctrine of promissory estoppel as an exception to the Statute of Frauds. Promissory estoppel is explained as:

A promise which the promisor should reasonably expect to induce action or forbearance on the part of the promisee or a third person and which does induce such action or forbearance is binding if injustice can be avoided only by enforcement of the promise. The remedy granted for breach may be limited as justice requires.

Amacher v. Brown–Forman Corp., 826 S.W.2d 480, 482 (Tenn.App.1991) (quoting *Restatement (Second) of Contracts* § 90); *see also Alden v. Presley* 637 S.W.2d 862, 864 (Tenn.1982).

There are limits to the application of promissory estoppel:

Detrimental action or forbearance by the promisee in reliance on a gratuitous promise, within limits constitutes a substitute for consideration, or a sufficient reason for enforcement of the promise without consideration. This doctrine is known as promissory estoppel. A promisor who induces substantial change of position by the promisee in reliance on the promise is estopped to deny its enforceability as lacking consideration. The reason for the doctrine is to avoid an unjust result, and its reason defines its limits. No injustice results in refusal to enforce a gratuitous promise where the loss suffered in reliance is negligible, nor where the promisee's action in reliance was unreasonable or unjustified by the promise. The limits of promissory estoppel are: (1) the detriment suffered in reliance must be substantial in an economic sense; (2) the substantial loss to the promisee in acting in reliance must have been foreseeable by the promisor; (3) the promisee must have acted reasonable in justifiable reliance on the promise as made.

Alden 637 S.W.2d at 864 (citing L. Simpson, Law of Contracts § 61 (2d ed. 1965)).

The doctrine of promissory estoppel is also referred to as "detrimental reliance" because the plaintiff must show not only that a promise was made, but also that the plaintiff reasonably relied on the promise to his detriment. Furthermore the promise upon which the promisee relied must be unambiguous and not unenforceably vague. However, a "claim of promissory estoppel is not dependent upon the existence of an expressed contract between the parties". . . .

From our review of the record, we conclude that there are disputes of material fact as to the alleged promises of defendant, the plaintiff's action and response thereto, and any inferences that legitimately may be drawn therefrom. The trier of fact should first determine whether a valid contract exists between the parties. In this regard, our Supreme Court stated in *Johnson v. Central Nat'l Ins. Co.,* 210 Tenn. 24, 356 S.W.2d 277 (1962):

> While a contract may be either expressed or implied, or written or oral, it must result from a meeting of the minds of the parties in mutual assent to the terms, must be based upon a sufficient consideration, free from fraud or undue influence, not against public policy and sufficiently definite to be enforced. *American Lead Pencil Company v. Nashville, Chattanooga & St. Louis Ry. Co.,* 124 Tenn. 57, 134 S.W. 613, 32 L.R.A., N.S., 323.

Id. at 281.

Alternatively, the trier of fact should determine whether plaintiff may rely upon the theory of promissory estoppel.

Accordingly, the order of the trial court granting summary judgment is reversed and this case is remanded for such further proceedings as necessary. Costs of appeal are assessed to appellee.

Notes and Questions

1. What do you think? If you were the judge in this case, what would you do? Do you think the elements for a valid, enforceable contract were present in this case? Would you enforce this promise with legal sanctions, or would you conclude that this type of promise is best handled by some other institution or government such as the family or the church?

2. Promissory Estoppel. Promissory estoppel or detrimental reliance is a concept that is used to enforce a promise upon which someone has detrimentally relied, even when, for some reason or another, the elements for a valid, enforceable contract are not present. What elements were possibly missing or what defense could possibly have been raised in this case that would make promissory estoppel necessary for Hope to get the assistance of the civil magistrate in enforcing this promise?

That said, is promissory estoppel consistent with the Christian worldview of contracts discussed earlier? In other words, if the elements for a valid, enforceable contract are not met, should the civil magistrate always refuse to act? What do you think justice demands? *See Exodus* 23:1-9; *Leviticus* 19:15; and *Deuteronomy* 1:16-17.

After you have considered these questions for yourself, read Professor Bern's analysis of a similar hypothetical at Roger Bern, *Biblical Model* at 136-138. Do you agree or disagree with Professor Bern's analysis? Compare this with Judge Posner's ideas concerning consideration and promissory estoppel or detrimental reliance found in § 4.2 of his *Economic Analysis of Law* (9th ed. 2014).

3. Other Christian Worldview Issues in the Contracts Setting. Obviously, the role or jurisdiction of the civil magistrate is a very important consideration in contracts law. You will also see other important Christian worldview issues or principles as you study contracts law including the sanctity of the promise, the voluntariness of committing oneself to a promise, and the importance of the right to and freedom of contract to economic liberty.

II. Sanctity of Promises

An important Christian worldview principle in the law of contracts is that promises are sacred. Since promises are sacred, certain types of promises are subject to enforcement by the civil magistrate. The importance of the sanctity of promises in society should lead us naturally to ask from where does this sacredness or sanctity come?

In the following famous case, Chief Justice John Marshall discusses the issue of the origins of contract law. Specifically, he is addressing whether the right to enter into contracts and have them enforced comes from the civil government or from the way God made things. While the language is older and can therefore be difficult, it is worth the effort. (To aid you in this worthy endeavor, I have used a number of footnotes in this opinion to offer some commentary on Justice Marshall's text modeled something after the way commentators use notes to explain and expound upon the biblical text in a study Bible.)

Justice Marshall was a fantastic leader on the Supreme Court who shaped early American law. He was gifted at bringing people over to his way of thinking, and during his long years on the court he wrote only a handful a dissenting opinions (in other words, he was almost always in the majority.) However, he felt the issues in the following case, one of which is the origin of contracts, to be so important that he dissented to set forth his views. As you read the opinion, consider where the right to enter into contracts and have them enforced comes from—the civil government or the Creator God? Also, consider why Justice Marshall thought the answer to this question to be so important. Finally, consider how this differs from Judge Posner's views on these important topics, and how these differing views might impact all of contract law.

Ogden v. Saunders
25 U.S. 213, 344-57 (1827)

Mr. Chief Justice MARSHALL [writing in dissent for himself and Justices Duvall and Story]

. . .

Contract, it is said, being the creature of society, derives its obligation from the law; and, although the law may not enter into the agreement so as to form a constituent part of it, still it acts externally upon the contract, and determines how far the principle of coercion shall be applied to it; and this being universally understood, no individual can complain justly of its application to himself, in a case where it was known when the contract was formed.

. . .

The defendants maintain that an error lies at the very foundation of this argument. It assumes that contract is the mere creature of society, and derives all its obligation from human legislation. That it is not the stipulation an individual makes which binds him, but some declaration of the supreme power of a State to which he belongs, that he shall perform what he has undertaken to perform. That though this original declaration may be lost in remote antiquity, it must be presumed as the origin of the obligation of contracts. This postulate the defendants deny, and, we think, with great reason.[45]

It is an argument of no inconsiderable weight against it, that we find no trace of such an enactment. So far back as human research carries us, we find the judicial power as a part of the executive, administering justice by the application of remedies to violated rights, or broken contracts. We find that

---

[45] Editor's Note: Justice Marshall is here noting that the argument forwarded by the defendants, and to some measure adopted by the majority opinion, is that contract law is essentially positive law only, i.e., it derives its origin, support, and power from the state or the civil magistrate, or, as Justice Marshall puts it, society. This is as opposed to contract law finding its origin, support, and power in the law of nature and nature's God, to borrow a phrase from the Declaration of Independence. Justice Marshall believes it to be the latter and not the former, as the opinion makes clear. Judge Posner, like Justice Holmes before him, would argue that contract law indeed is found only in the state or "society."

power applying these remedies on the idea of a pre-existing obligation on every man to do what he has promised on consideration to do; that the breach of this obligation is an injury for which the injured party has a just claim to compensation, and that society ought to afford him a remedy for that injury. We find allusions to the mode of acquiring property, but we find no allusion, from the earliest time, to any supposed act of the governing power giving obligation to contracts. On the contrary, the proceedings respecting them of which we know any thing, evince the idea of a pre-existing intrinsic obligation which human law enforces. If, on tracing the right to contract, and the obligations created by contract, to their source, we find them to exist anterior to, and independent of society, we may reasonably conclude that those original and pre-existing principles are, like many other natural rights, brought with man into society; and, although they may be controlled, are not given by human legislation.[46]

In the rudest state of nature[47] a man governs himself, and labours for his own purposes. That which he acquires is his own, at least while in his possession, and he may transfer it to another. This transfer passes his right to that other. Hence the right to barter. One man may have acquired more skins than are necessary for his protection from the cold; another more food than is necessary for his immediate use. They agree each to supply the wants of the other from his surplus. Is this contract without obligation? If one of them, having received and eaten the food he needed, refuses to deliver the skin, may not the other rightfully compel him to deliver it? Or two persons agree to unite their strength and skill to hunt together for their mutual advantage,

---

[46] Editor's Note: In other words, the United States federal government nor the government of the Commonwealth of Virginia endow me with the right to enter into contracts. Rather, Marshall argues, that right is mine inherently. Again, to borrow a phrase from the Declaration of Independence, we might say that I have been endowed by my Creator with certain inalienable rights, among which is the right to bind myself to contracts and to seek to have contracts to which I am a party enforced. Generally speaking, law and economics scholars, such as Judge Posner, reject any idea of inherent, inalienable rights granted by the Creator. Rather, rights would be something granted by the state as the highest sovereign.

[47] Editor's Note: Justice Marshall is here referring to a simpler state of affairs and societal organization where there is little or no functioning civil government. For example, in the book of *Genesis* in *The Bible,* there is very little civil government to which the patriarchs are subject prior to entering Egypt. Abraham, Isaac, and Jacob appear largely to have been governed by self-government and family government, and, while they interacted with certain civil governments (such as Abimelech of the Philistines,) they appeared to be only loosely subject to such governments. *See, e.g., Genesis* 13 (Abraham and Lot enter into an agreement to separate that both assumed would be binding), 21:22-34 (Abraham and Abimelech, a Philistine ruler, enter into a treaty), 23 (Abraham enters into a contract to purchase the field in Machpelah from Ephron as a burial place for Sarah), 25:29-24 (Esau enters into an agreement with Jacob to transfer Jacob his birthright in exchange for some stew), 26:6-33 (Isaac and Abimelech enter into an agreement similar to the one that Abraham entered into with the Philistines), and 28-31 (Jacob enters into a series of agreements with Laban). (It is worthy to note that, in many of these early "contracts," it appears that the only authority that could be called upon to enforce them was the family or perhaps only the Lord Himself, presumably because there was no civil magistrate to which all parties were subject.) Accordingly, by looking at this "rudest state of nature" and finding binding contracts, Justice Marshall is going to make the argument that the right to contract, therefore, precedes organized civil "society" and therefore inures in the nature of mankind.

engaging to divide the animal they shall master. Can one of them rightfully take the whole? or, should he attempt it, may not the other force him to a division? If the answer to these questions must affirm the duty of keeping faith between these parties, and the right to enforce it if violated, the answer admits the obligation of contracts, because, upon that obligation depends the right to enforce them. Superior strength may give the power, but cannot give the right. The rightfulness of coercion must depend on the pre-existing obligation to do that for which compulsion is used.[48] It is no objection to the principle, that the injured party may be the weakest. In society, the wrong-doer may be too powerful for the law. He may deride its coercive power, yet his contracts are obligatory; and, if society acquire the power of coercion, that power will be applied without previously enacting that his contract is obligatory.

Independent nations are individuals in a state of nature. Whence is derived the obligation of their contracts? They admit the existence of no superior legislative power which is to give them validity, yet their validity is acknowledged by all. If one of these contracts be broken, all admit the right of the injured party to demand reparation for the injury, and to enforce that reparation if it be withheld. He may not have the power to enforce it, but the whole civilized world concurs in saying, that the power, if possessed, is rightfully used.[49]

In a state of nature, these individuals may contract, their contracts are obligatory, and force may rightfully be employed to coerce the party who has broken his engagement.

What is the effect of society upon these rights? When men unite together and form a government, do they surrender their right to contract, as well as their right to enforce the observance of contracts? ... [I]ndividuals do not derive from government their right to contract, but bring that right with them into society; that obligation is not conferred on contracts by positive law, but is intrinsic, and is conferred by the act of the parties. This results from the right which every man retains to acquire property, to dispose of that property according to his own judgment, and to pledge himself for a future act. These rights are not given by society, but are brought into it. The right of coercion is necessarily surrendered to government, and this surrender imposes on government the correlative duty of furnishing a remedy.[50] The right to

---

[48] Editor's Note: Justice Marshall powerfully demonstrates that law and the coercive power thereof requires more than just might or naked power. In order for there to be justice, the coercive power of the law must be coupled with a right. In this case, the right is the right to enter into contracts and have them enforced. Again, contra to the positivist position, Justice Marshall sees this right as deriving from the law of nature and nature's God, as opposed to only from the civil government. By contrast, Justice Holmes, Judge Posner, and most law and economics scholars take the positivist approach.

[49] Editor's Note: *See* the treaties referenced earlier between the rulers of the Philistines and Abraham and later Isaac as examples.

[50] Editor's Note: Marshall is here referring to the so-called "power of the sword" that the civil magistrate wields, which means that only the civil magistrate may use this coercive power on other people. I may not enforce a contract myself by imposing a fine on my neighbor who I believe

regulate contracts, to prescribe rules by which they shall be evidenced, to prohibit such as may be deemed mischievous, is unquestionable, and has been universally exercised. So far as this power has restrained the original right of individuals to bind themselves by contract, it is restrained; but beyond these actual restraints the original power remains unimpaired.

This reasoning is, undoubtedly, much strengthened by the authority of those writers on natural and national law, whose opinions have been viewed with profound respect by, the wisest men of the present, and of past ages.

Notes and Questions

1. Ultimate Origins of Contract Law. Justice Marshall clearly believed that the right to and obligation of contract is derived not from the civil magistrate but rather from the law of nature and nature's God. He argues that this right and obligation is bound up in the nature of mankind. Do you agree? Do you think that the right to and obligation of contract is more than just a positive law of the state? Would Judge Posner agree? What would he say in response do you think?

Assuming that Justice Marshall is right and that something about the very nature of mankind gives rise to the right to contract, where did that right come from? To state it differently, why is the right to contract a part of the inherent rights of man? As discussed previously, I would submit that it is derived from mankind's stewardship-dominion duties and the image of God in man. God is a promise-making and promise-keeping God. The Bible is full of and centers around God's promises to mankind and His keeping of those promises, most ultimately of course in the Lord Jesus Christ. Accordingly, as humans, we bear the image of God and, like our Creator, we can bind ourselves to contracts and, when we do, we are obligated to keep them. Accordingly, the ultimate source and origin of contract law is found in the nature of God Himself.

2. The Contracts Clause. The Founding Fathers clearly felt that the right to and enforcement of contracts was very important. Article I, Section 10, Clause 1 of the United States Constitution provides that "No State shall . . . pass any Law impairing the Obligation of Contracts." This clause was at issue in *Ogden v. Saunders* (in a portion of the opinion edited out.) Further, in the famous case of *Fletcher v. Peck*, 10 U.S. 87 (1810), Chief Justice John Marshall, writing for a six-to-one majority, declared a Georgia law unconstitutional because it violated the Contracts Clause. For an interesting discussion of the Contracts Clause and its decline in importance in recent years, *see* James W. Ely, Jr., *Whatever Happened to the Contracts Clause?*, 4 Charleston L. Rev. 371 (2010). As Professor Ely points out, the Contracts Clause was once one of the most important provisions in the Constitution for limiting the power of the civil

---

to have breached his agreement with me. Rather, I must petition the civil magistrate for redress. The civil magistrate bears the sword as God's avenger; I do not. *See Romans* 12:19-13:5.

magistrate. Why do you think that a clause that was so important to the Founders and so important in the early centuries of the Republic has fallen into such disfavor and disuse in the twentieth and twenty-first centuries?

3. *Sacredness of Promises.* Since God makes and keeps His promises, He (and derivatively other people) expects us to keep our promises. We therefore can say that contracts are sacred because God expects us to fulfill what we promise. *See, e.g., Numbers* 30:2, *Deuteronomy* 23:21, and *Ecclesiastes* 5:1-7.

Since promises are sacred, contracts, as a subset of promises that are enforceable by the civil government, are also sacred. Therefore, a just civil government would seek to encourage contract-keeping and punish or discourage contract-breaking. Not surprisingly, a society that has a history of making and keeping promises and contracts is a blessed society. Its commerce will be more robust making all members better off, and its community will be stronger. This should be expected because we know that God's commands are not burdensome but are rather for our good. *See* 1 John 5:2-3.

Americans used to view promises as sacred. We used to be a faithful society, but in many ways we are, or are becoming, a faithless society. We used to be a society where one's promise or word was one's bond—it meant something. If someone agreed to do something, they felt very strongly that they should keep their promise. Handshake deals used to be common because a person's handshake meant that he had bound himself and would keep his promise.

Unfortunately, our society has departed from this level of integrity and we no longer see ourselves bound by our word. This shows up in a number of ways and examples are so numerous as to make examples unnecessary. In many ways, we have become a society of liars. It has undermined our trust in each other, and it is already and will continue to have enormous negative effects on our commerce and communities.

However, before rushing to judge others, it is helpful to consider our own hearts. Keeping your word is often difficult, and we may share our societal predilection for keeping our word only when it is easy and benefits us. In that regard, consider the following example.

In discussing the fact that we have become a faithless society that does not keep its word, Larry Burkett in *Business by the Book*, relates this example:

> I recall a time when my father, who was an electrician, agreed to rewire a neighbor's house for about $2,000. In the midst of the job he found that he had underbid by several hundred dollars and, at the same time, the cost of materials jumped because of a copper shortage. On a $2,000 job, my father stood to lose nearly $1,200, a sizable sum in the early fifties.

Larry Burkett, *Business By The Book: Complete Guide of Biblical Principles for the Workplace* 75 (2006). What would you do in a situation like this? Would you keep your word and fulfill the contract, or would you look to get out of the deal? What would *The Bible* say about how to handle this situation? *See Psalm* 15:1-5. (By the way, Larry Burkett's dad kept his word.)[51]

4. Keeping Your Word. *The Bible* clearly indicates that Christians should be people of the truth. We should keep our word and fulfill our vows. *See, e.g., Exodus* 20:16, *Leviticus* 19:11, *Psalm* 15:1-4 and 58:3, *Proverbs* 6:16-19, *Ecclesiastes* 5:4-7, *Matthew* 5:33-37, *Ephesians* 4:25, and *Colossians* 3:9. However, often we all get busy in life and things sneak up on us. Therefore, it is good to plan in advance to do certain things and perhaps implement certain policies that will help us to keep our word and not overcommit or otherwise get in a situation where we are looking to "get out of" promises that we have made. We want to see these principles (i.e., the sacredness of the promise) reflected in our legal system, and we, therefore, need to live our lives in such a way that we, and organizations that we have control over, reflect these principles. For example, Larry Burkett suggests several guidelines for helping us to keep our word in *Business by the Book* such as "when in doubt, say no" and "don't book too far ahead." Can you think of others? How would you go about creating a culture of promise-keeping in your family or any organization where you work or have authority?

III. Is There a Moral Obligation to Perform Contracts?

Throughout this chapter, we have assumed that a moral obligation exists to keep one's word. We have assumed that there is a certain sacredness about promises in general and contracts in particular and that they should therefore be fulfilled. Obviously, *The Bible* clearly teaches that promises should be kept in a number of verses. *See, e.g., Exodus* 20:16, *Leviticus* 19:11, *Psalm* 15:1-4 and 58:3, *Proverbs* 6:16-19, *Ecclesiastes* 5:4-7, *Matthew* 5:33-37, *Ephesians* 4:25, and *Colossians* 3:9. Further, it seems that virtually every child, at a very young age, assumes that promises made to them should be kept. As a father of nine, I have had one of my children say to another on many occasions—"Hey, you promised!"[52]

Given the ubiquity of the idea that there is generally some level of moral obligation to keep one's word, you might think that all legal scholars and jurisprudes work under those same assumptions that we have made throughout this chapter. After all, even children live and work under these assumptions. However, you would be wrong. In fact, the most influential jurisprudential thought system in America today, law and economics, rejects

---

[51] This is just one of many great examples that Larry Burkett gives in his book of how hard it can be to keep our word. They are certainly worth reading and reflecting upon.

[52] Of course, children are born with a sin nature in addition to some understanding of God's requirements. *See Romans* 1:18-3:18. Therefore, just like us, they are quick to hold others to the requirements of the law but slower to be willing to fulfill the law themselves. Such is the heritage we have from our father Adam—praise God we have a different one in Christ! *Romans* 5:12-21.

the so-called moral theory of contract law (the one we have been working under) in favor of what they refer to as the option theory of contract law.

Law and economics scholars, such as Judge Posner, view the greatest good that the legal system should be seeking as economic efficiency. They don't see a place for moral theory or talk of moral obligations in the law, as many Americans would assume. Accordingly, like American legal realists, such as Justice Oliver Wendell Holmes, Jr., before them, they view contracts as merely options, not as moral obligations. Therefore, they conclude that, when it is efficient to do so, one should break his word and breach his contract and just pay damages. Judge Posner describes it this way:

> Many students of contract law believe that because a contract is a promise, breaking a contract, at least if it is done deliberately (remember that many breaches of contract are involuntary), is a wrongful act. Those who hold this view are apt to think that the remedies for breach of contract are inadequate.
>
> But is it a sound view? Oliver Wendell Holmes argued, in the spirit of positive economics, that contracts are options— when you sign a contract in which you promise a specified performance (supplying a product or providing a service), you buy an option to perform or pay damages. . . . As long as you pay the damages awarded by the court in the promisee's suit for breach of contract, whether they are specified in the clause or computed according to the principles of contract damages, no blame can attach to your not performing, even if it was deliberate—even if, for example, you did not perform simply because someone offered you more money for the product or service that you had undertaken to supply in the contract, and you lacked the capacity to supply both the promisee and the new, more necessitous customer. You have not really broken your promise, because what you promised (though that is not how the contract will have been worded) was either-or: not performance but either performance or compensation for the cost of nonperformance to the other party to the contract.
>
> The option theory is thus a "no-fault" theory of contract law.[53]

As the foregoing demonstrates, law and economics posits a "no-fault" theory of contract law that makes it so no one is ever guilty of breaking his

---

[53] Posner, *Economic Analysis of Law* 170 (quoting Oliver W. Holmes, *The Path of the Law*, 10 Harv. L. Rev. 457, 462 (1897)). Oliver W. Holmes has a near semi-divine status in American jurisprudence, but most Americans even today would find his worldview disturbing. For more on Justice Holmes and his worldview, *see* Rodney D. Chrisman, *Holmes the Monster*, www.RodneyChrisman.com   (January   28,   2011), http://www.rodneychrisman.com/2011/01/28/holmes-the-monster/.

word by breaching a contract. The contract may be written that way, but in fact it does not say what it means. What it really means is an option—perform or pay damages. Morality and fulfilling commitments has nothing to do with it, at least according to Judge Posner.

Christians, and indeed most scholars throughout the history of the Western legal tradition, have reached a different conclusion working from an entirely different premise. Working from a premise that there is a moral obligation to keep one's word and that this moral obligation is relevant to contract law, Christian scholars reach a conclusion very different from Posner's. Professor Bern's analysis from his exceptional *Biblical Model* article, cited earlier in this chapter, is an excellent example of Christian thinking on this topic.

> *A* promises to purchase raw materials for use in his manufacturing business from *B* for a price, and *B* promises in return to sell them to *A* at that price. Thereafter, and before *A* has changed his position in reliance on the promise, *B* breaks his promise to *A* and sells them at a higher price to *C*. *A* sues, requesting appropriate relief for the breach.
>
> Under the Biblical Model analysis, *B*'s conduct of breaking his promise under these circumstances would, at the very least, appear to be sin for which he is accountable to God. That fact alone, however, serious as it is, does not mean that the breach is within the jurisdiction of Civil Government. The additional inquiry must be made as to whether *B*'s conduct in this instance is such as to put him in the category of an evildoer with respect to which Civil Government has jurisdiction to act.
>
> In pursuing that inquiry, recall that under the stewardship-dominion mandate *A* is under a duty to steward to the glory of God all of his time, talent and resources. *B* is under a duty to God to recognize that duty and not to interfere with *A*'s carrying it out. By his words of promise, *B* created an expectation in *A* that his assistance in *A*'s stewardship-dominion activity would be forthcoming and has now dashed that expectation. Not only has *A*'s expectation been disappointed, but the transaction costs (including time, effort, and potential foregone opportunities) inherent in putting the *A-B* agreement together have been wasted. Additional transaction costs will be incurred when *A* arranges a substitute transaction or otherwise alters his business operations to accommodate not having the raw materials, to say nothing of the transaction costs in endeavoring to obtain redress from *B* for the disruption he has caused. These adverse effects confirm

that *B*'s actions have interfered with *A*'s efforts to carry out his stewardship-dominion duties to God and constitute evildoing (*kakos*) with respect to which Civil Government has jurisdiction. Additionally, such actions, if unchecked by Civil Government, also threaten the sanctity of promise and its continued effectiveness as a unique vehicle for enhancing stewardship-dominion capabilities.

This position is, of course, contrary to that of the proponents of law and economics analysis who advocate the "efficient breach" theory. The premise for such analysis is the non-Biblical proposition that the greatest good is achieved by actions which facilitate the movement of goods and services to their highest and best use, judged by the willingness, at a particular point in time, of people to pay for them. According to that analysis, because *C* is willing to pay more for the materials now than *A* had previously agreed to pay, *B* should break his promise to *A* and sell them to *C* if, after *B* pays *A*'s damages, *B* will have a larger profit and the materials will be in the hands of the one who presumably has a more valuable use for them.

Apart from its non-Biblical premise, which undermines the planning benefit that is one of the key individual and societal gains from agreement, the efficient breach theory is patently deficient in other respects.[54]

Professor Bern then goes on to explain at least four reasons why the efficient breach theory is a bad idea, beyond its undermining the sanctity of promise and its non-biblical premise. They are: (1) Efficient breach theory is deficient, even under its own premises, in that "it does not attempt to measure all of the costs inherent in the transaction in determining whether the overall wealth of society is increased or decreased by the breach."[55] (2) "[E]fficient breach theory ignores the reality that the remedies system, pursuant to which *A*'s damages will be measured, is grossly undercompensatory."[56] (3)"[T]he instances in which an 'efficient breach' can occur are most limited. They occur only in instances of market distortion such that *C* is willing to pay greater than market price for the materials."[57] (4) "[E]ven if one were to accept the premise that society will be better off if the materials in the Illustration end up in *C*'s hands, there are ways to accomplish that other than by *B*'s breach."[58]

---

[54] Bern, *Biblical Model* 132-34 (citations omitted).

[55] *Id.* at 134.

[56] *Id.* Professor Bern writes more on remedies in this article at pages 159-173.

[57] *Id.* at 134-135.

[58] *Id.* at 135.

Notes and Questions

1. What Do You Think? Do you find yourself more in agreement with Professor Bern or Judge Posner? Should we really attempt to understand the law apart from any moral standards? Can we? What do you think?

2. Performance or Damages, Which Would You Prefer? Let's imagine you engage in a common Internet commerce transaction such as buying an item on eBay. Do you view the contract that is made when you win the bid as being an option? In other words, do you understand the transaction that you just entered into to be such that the other party can either send you the item as agreed or just choose not to and pay the damages to you? Would you be just as satisfied with the damages? Would you think that the other person had wronged you if he broke his word and didn't ship the item?

If efficient breach theory is correct, and contracts really are just options, then it seems that you should be indifferent as between the outcomes above. You should be equally satisfied with performance or damages. However, most people probably don't feel that way. Further, if this idea were to become widespread, it would undermine the trust that is necessary for commercial activity.

Think about it for a moment. When we order things online from Amazon.com or Ebay, we are placing a significant amount of trust in these companies and the sellers (if it is a different party.) This trust makes it very efficient for people to enter into these types of transactions, and, as Professor Bern points out, voluntary agreements are very useful in helping us to fulfill the stewardship-dominion mandate. This trust exists, in part, because there is a widely recognized moral obligation to keep one's word. Accordingly, undermining that trust by eroding the moral obligation at its foundation would eventually have serious consequences for commercial activity and, contra the law and economics position, would actually make everyone worse off.

3. Damages Inadequate? Professor Bern thinks that contract damages and remedies are inadequate. Judge Posner seems to disagree. What do you think? Are they inadequate? If so, what should they be?

IV. Voluntariness of Contracts

Jones v. Star Credit Corp.
298 N.Y.S.2d 264, 6 UCC Rep.Serv. 76 (1969)

On August 31, 1965 the plaintiffs, who are welfare recipients, agreed to purchase a home freezer unit for $900 as the result of a visit from a salesman representing Your Shop At Home Service, Inc. With the addition of the time credit charges, credit life insurance, credit property insurance, and sales tax, the purchase price totaled $1,234.80. Thus far the plaintiffs have paid $619.88 toward their purchase. The defendant claims that with various added credit charges paid for an extension of time there is a balance of $819.81 still due from the plaintiffs. The uncontroverted proof at the trial established that the freezer unit, when purchased, had a maximum retail value of approximately $300. The question is whether this transaction and the resulting contract could be considered unconscionable within the meaning of Section 2—302 of the Uniform Commercial Code which provides in part:

> (1) If the court as a matter of law finds the contract or any clause of the contract to have been unconscionable at the time it was made the court may refuse to enforce the contract, or it may enforce the remainder of the contract without the unconscionable clause, or it may so limit the application of any unconscionable clause as to avoid any unconscionable result.

> (2) When it is claimed or appears to the court that the contract or any clause thereof may be unconscionable the parties shall be afforded a reasonable opportunity to present evidence as to its commercial setting, purpose and effect to aid the court in making the determination.

There was a time when the shield of 'caveat emptor' would protect the most unscrupulous in the marketplace—a time when the law, in granting parties unbridled latitude to make their own contracts, allowed exploitive and callous practices which shocked the conscience of both legislative bodies and the courts.

The effort to eliminate these practices has continued to pose a difficult problem. On the one hand it is necessary to recognize the importance of preserving the integrity of agreements and the fundamental right of parties to deal, trade, bargain, and contract. On the other hand there is the concern for the uneducated and often illiterate individual who is the victim of gross inequality of bargaining power, usually the poorest members of the community.

Concern for the protection of these consumers against overreaching by the small but hardy breed of merchants who would prey on them is not novel. The dangers of inequality of bargaining power were vaguely recognized in the early English common law when Lord Hardwicke wrote of a fraud, which "may be apparent from the intrinsic nature and subject of the bargain itself; such as no man in his senses and not under delusion would make." The English authorities on this subject were discussed in *Hume v. United States*, 132 U.S. 406, 411, 10 S.Ct. 134, 136, 33 L.Ed. 393 (1889) where the United States Supreme Court characterized these as "cases in which one party took advantage of the other's ignorance of arithmetic to impose upon him, and the fraud was apparent from the face of the contracts."

The law is beginning to fight back against those who once took advantage of the poor and illiterate without risk of either exposure or interference. From the common law doctrine of intrinsic fraud we have, over the years, developed common and statutory law which tells not only the buyer but also the seller to beware. This body of laws recognizes the importance of a free enterprise system but at the same time will provide the legal armor to protect and safeguard the prospective victim from the harshness of an unconscionable contract.

Section 2—302 of the Uniform Commercial Code enacts the moral sense of the community into the law of commercial transactions. It authorizes the court to find, as a matter of law, that a contract or a clause of a contract was "unconscionable at the time it was made," and upon so finding the court may refuse to enforce the contract, excise the objectionable clause or limit the application of the clause to avoid an unconscionable result. "The principle," states the Official Comment to this section, "is one of the prevention of oppression and unfair surprise." It permits a court to accomplish directly what heretofore was often accomplished by construction of language, manipulations of fluid rules of contract law and determinations based upon a presumed public policy.

There is no reason to doubt, moreover, that this section is intended to encompass the price term of an agreement. In addition to the fact that it has already been so applied, the statutory language itself makes it clear that not only a clause of the contract, but the contract *in toto*, may be found unconscionable as a matter of law. Indeed, no other provision of an agreement more intimately touches upon the question of unconscionability than does the term regarding price.

Fraud, in the instant case, is not present; nor is it necessary under the statute. The question which presents itself is whether or not, under the circumstances of this case, the sale of a freezer unit having a retail value of $300 for $900 ($1,439.69 including credit charges and $18 sales tax) is unconscionable as a matter of law. The court believes it is.

Concededly, deciding the issue is substantially easier than explaining it. No doubt, the mathematical disparity between $300, which presumably includes a reasonable profit margin, and $900, which is exorbitant on its face, carries the greatest weight. Credit charges alone exceed by more than $100 the retail value of the freezer. These alone, may be sufficient to sustain the decision. Yet, a caveat is warranted lest we reduce the import of Section 2—302 solely to a mathematical ratio formula. It may, at times, be that; yet it may also be much more. The very limited financial resources of the purchaser, known to the sellers at the time of the sale, is entitled to weight in the balance. Indeed, the value disparity itself leads inevitably to the felt conclusion that knowing advantage was taken of the plaintiffs. In addition, the meaningfulness of choice essential to the making of a contract can be negated by a gross inequality of bargaining power.

There is no question about the necessity and even the desirability of installment sales and the extension of credit. Indeed, there are many, including welfare recipients, who would be deprived of even the most basic conveniences without the use of these devices. Similarly, the retail merchant

> Israel went yearly to lament the daughter of Jephthah the Gileadite four days in a year.[59]

Commentators disagree over whether Jephthah had to actually offer his daughter up as a burnt offering, or whether she simply remained a virgin for all of her life. Either would have been tragic for both. Regardless, it clearly makes the point that vows to God, and by extension vows to our fellowman, should be taken very seriously, even if it is a "bad deal."

Dean Titus argues that: since man is not obligated to make vows or promises to God or his fellowman, i.e., he has freedom to abstain from vows or promises, he is bound by his words when he does make a vow or promise. Herbert W. Titus, *God, Man, and Law: The Biblical Principles* 219 (1994). In discussing this idea, Dean Titus addresses Jephthah's tragic vow as follows: "Jephthah's vow to sacrifice the first one out of his house to meet him after victory over Israel's enemy was binding even though its fulfillment required the putting to death of Jephthah's daughter, a clear violation of God's law against murder." *Id.*

This is, admittedly, a very difficult Bible passage to understand. However, it seems to clearly teach both the sacredness of promises and their voluntariness (in that Jephthah was not required to make this vow), if nothing else, in a graphic and tragic way. This teaching lines up with *The Bible*'s other teachings on this topic. *See, e.g., Exodus* 20:16, *Leviticus* 19:11, *Psalm* 15:1-4 and 58:3, *Proverbs* 6:16-19, *Ecclesiastes* 5:4-7, *Matthew* 5:33-37, *Ephesians* 4:25, and *Colossians* 3:9. What do you think? Does this Bible story and the related principle that our promises are sacred and must be kept, even in very difficult situations, shed any light on whether this case was rightly decided?

5. Is this Justice? It is often said that "bad facts make bad law." Certainly, this was a tough deal for the plaintiffs. However, does that fact alone mean that the court was in the right to rule as it did? Did the court consider things that should not be considered when administering justice? *See Exodus* 23:1-9; *Leviticus* 19:15; and *Deuteronomy* 1:16-17.

6. Professor Bern on Jones v. Star Credit Corp. Professor Bern used the facts of this case as Illustration 8 in his *Biblical Model* article. His comments are very helpful.

> Unconscionability is a defense recognized by both the Uniform Commercial Code and Restatement (Second) of Contracts. Neither provision provides a definition of "unconscionability," and all authorities agree the term is undefinable. The concept is typically said to include "an absence of meaningful choice on the part of one of the parties together with contract terms which are unreasonably favorable to the other party."

---

[59] A famous painting by Sir John Everett Millais depicts Jephthah being comforted by his daughter after making this tragic vow.

Factors of status, behavior and substance often combine in the court's assessment of whether there was an absence of meaningful choice or whether the terms were unduly favorable to one of the parties. In the cases in which the unconscionability defense is asserted, the behavior factor itself is insufficient to raise a defense consistent with Biblical principles. Rather the behavior, (e.g., the sales pitch used, or the way terms were worded or presented in written documents) is usually posited to have significance because of the social, educational or economic status of the promisor, or because of a perceived disparity in the substance of the transaction.

Under the Model analysis, it appears that both the status factor and the substance factor are contrary to Biblical principles. Considering the economic, social, and educational status of the litigants, and favoring the weaker party is inconsistent with the *mishpat* requisite for the proper administration of justice. That feature of impartial and even-handed treatment of all without regard to social or financial status is impossible to implement when the status of the litigants is one of the two most significant factors to consider in applying the defense.

Consideration of the substance of the transaction and whether it appears to be unreasonably one-sided is also improper under the Model analysis. Civil Government does not act within its authority when it dictates directly or indirectly the terms upon which parties can or cannot contract, save to the extent of prohibiting bargains to accomplish purposes antithetical to the creation order. If Civil Government attempts to limit or proscribe the substance of what parties might otherwise independently agree upon in otherwise lawful bargains, it acts not in its authorized role as an avenger against evildoers, but rather in a dominion role which has never been assigned to it.

Civil Government is not the recipient of the dominion-mandate, nor is there anything in Scripture to suggest that it is a better judge of what value an article or service has for an individual than is the individual himself. Yet that is the message communicated when Civil Government interposes its judgment that the individual agreed to pay too much. When Civil Government does so, it sends a very negative message about the worth of the individual, or a category of individuals, i.e., that their personal judgments about the worth of an item and the pleasure it will bring to them are unworthy of recognition by Civil Government. It also sends a clear message that such an individual is not responsible for making improvident stewardship-dominion decisions because the Civil

Government, which is acting more in the role of a guardian than an avenger of evil, will relieve him of the obligation that his promise would ordinarily create.   In so doing, Civil Government undermines the creation order primacy of self-government, as well as the principle of individual accountability to God for stewardship-dominion decisions.

The combined effect of violation of the *mishpat* requisite (by favoring the poor and weak) and the usurpation of dominion authority suggests that in these instances Civil Government is really endeavoring to compel love by the merchant (by precluding him from collecting the promised amount) rather than to provide redress for evildoing. Although *A*, the ghetto merchant, may be motivated by greed and may be guilty of sin by not acting in a loving way toward *B* in pricing the freezer, his lack of charity is a sin before God alone, and does not in this instance trigger the jurisdiction of Civil Government.

Under the Model analysis, the appropriate inquiry is: has *A*, by setting the price at $900 (plus credit charges) on the freezer and encouraging *B* to purchase it, interfered with *B*'s carrying out his stewardship dominion duties to God?   The facts do not suggest that he has. *A* offered *B* the opportunity to make a choice about the freezer. *B* could choose to purchase at the price asked, try to negotiate a better price, or simply not purchase the freezer at all. *A* could not compel *B's* decision. As steward over his resources, *B* had the duty to exercise effective self-government in making that choice.

B's decision, the product of neither misrepresentation nor duress, appears to have been that having the freezer presently would be of more value and benefit to him than having $1,234 in cash available over the next several years to purchase other items or services.   If *B's* decision was not the exercise of good self-government and stewardship-dominion duties, that would be sin for which he is answerable to God. If it was a good exercise of his obligations to God, then God is pleased with his use of promise in this setting. In either case, *B's* breaking his promise to pay the full amount is not only sin, but also an act of evildoing as to *A* under the principles previously discussed in connection with Illustration 1.

The final point to be made takes us back to the acknowledged inability to define "unconscionability." Apart from all of the other problems with the defense previously addressed, the inherently definitionless nature of the defense makes clear that it represents a statement of feelings rather than a statement of a rule of law. Its standardless character obviously offends the *tsedeq* (righteous moral standard) feature of God's law and thus violates a requisite for human law and its proper administration. There can be no expectation that justice will be done in any case in which that feature is not operative.[60]

Are you convinced by Professor Bern's arguments that the unconscionability doctrine is actually unlawful from a biblical perspective? Why or why not? What does Judge Posner think? How does it compare with Professor Bern's opinion?

V. The Right to Contract and Economic Liberty

In previous sections, we considered the very important issue of the role of the civil magistrate in enforcing contracts. In order to do this, we considered the question "What is a contract?" We saw that this led us to a consideration of the elements of a valid, enforceable contract as a means of determining when a promise or set of promises rises to the level of a contract and therefore is subject to enforcement by the civil magistrate with legal sanctions.

Further, in previous sections, we saw that there are other important Christian worldview principles and issues that arise in contracts law. One such issue is the sanctity or sacredness of the promise. God views vows very seriously and does not suffer liars. *See, e.g., Numbers* 30:2, *Deuteronomy* 23:21, and *Ecclesiastes* 5:1-7. Accordingly, we should expect the legal system to have a very high view of the sacredness of promises. Another such issue is the voluntariness of contracts. God does not require that we make many vows, but, when we do make them, He expects us to fulfill them. Accordingly, an important Christian worldview issue in contracts law is voluntariness. Several elements, such as agreement and consideration address this from various angles and other doctrines, such as unconscionability, seem to undercut it.

And, lastly, a very important issue in contracts law is the freedom of or the right to contract. This is a liberty issue, and it builds on the idea of the origin of rights discussed in previous sections. Rights derive from our duties to God. We have a duty to use everything that God has given us—time, treasure, talents, etc.—for His glory. As we have seen previously, this can be referred to as the stewardship-dominion mandate or duties. Thus, based upon this duty that we owe God, we have a right to be free from the interference of others (other individuals, the family, the church, and the civil government) in the discharge of this duty. This gives rise to a particular type of liberty that is often overlooked in our time; I will refer to it herein as economic liberty, i.e., the right to use the resources that God has entrusted to me in the manner I see fit.

In this regard, it can be said that there are three broad categories of liberty: political liberty, religious liberty, and economic liberty. All three are

---

[60] Bern, *Biblical Model* 147-150.

very important, and a people enjoying all three at the same time is almost unheard of in history. In fact, it can be argued that the first (and only) time it ever occurred in the history of the world was at the era of the American founding.

At the time of the founding of America, the governmental system created by the Constitution and the various state and local governments served to diffuse the power of the civil government and limit it, to a large degree, to its proper biblical role or jurisdiction, as discussed to some degree in the previous sections. As the power of the civil magistrate (and particularly the federal or central government) has grown in America, these important liberties have been steadily eroded as the civil magistrate has grown beyond its God-given limitations. Indeed, the Constitutional Republic of the founding era hardly exists today, having been replaced with something much closer to a European-style socialist democracy than the carefully limited civil government envisioned by our nation's founders.

It is not discussed as often as the other liberties, but the Founders clearly believed that economic liberty was a very important God-given liberty. In fact, it is entirely possible that the phrase "the pursuit of happiness" used in the Declaration of Independence is a reference to the right to private property and economic liberty. This very important Christian worldview principle arises in contract law in the context of the freedom of or right to contract.

In order to protect the important right to fulfill our stewardship-dominion duties to God, the civil magistrate should have a disposition toward allowing people to have the freedom to or right to contract as they see fit and toward enforcing these contracts that people make without inquiry into the substance of the deal or forcing terms into the deal. Without being able to enter into contracts and seek their enforcement when they are breached, it becomes very difficult to engage in the type of economic activity that would allow us to glorify God with what He has entrusted to us. *See, e.g., Matthew* 25:14-30 and *Luke* 19:21-27. Thus, it becomes obvious that the right to contract, and the corollary right to have those contracts enforced according to the terms that the parties agreed to, is an essential component to economic liberty.[61]

However, as noted earlier, our liberties in America have been steadily eroded since the founding era. In fact, a strong argument could be made that our economic liberties have actually been eroded even more than the other liberties. Many examples abound. An example that is very much in the minds of many Americans at the time of the writing of this chapter is the healthcare reform act known as Obamacare. It requires that every American purchase a

---

[61] *See, e.g.*, Bern, *Biblical Model* 131-153, and Titus, *God, Man, and Law* 219-223. On the goodness of commercial activity in general, *see* Rodney D. Chrisman, *Can a Merchant Please God?: The Church's Historic Teaching on the Goodness of Just Commercial Activity as a Foundational Principle of Commercial Law Jurisprudence*, 6 Liberty U. L. Rev. 453 (2012) and Wayne Grudem, *Business for the Glory of God: The Bible's Teaching on the Moral Goodness of Business* (2003).

product—health insurance—or pay a penalty (or tax?).[62] That is an astounding encroachment by the civil magistrate onto our economic liberties.

As we shall see throughout the course, many of the encroachments on the freedom of contract and economic liberty are not so blatant and "in-your-face" as Obamacare. On the contrary, throughout our nation's history, they have often been more subtle, couched in terms of regulations and restrictions that few Americas know about.

The milk industry in America is a case in point. This industry is subject to an astounding array of regulations and controls such that economic freedom and the freedom to contract has been all but eliminated (and many Americans don't even know about these regulations and controls.) For example, the simple act of a farmer selling milk fresh from his cow is illegal in many states and regulated, to some degree, in all states. In other words and by way of illustration, in the Commonwealth of Virginia, where I live, it is illegal for me to contract to purchase a gallon of milk with a neighbor who owns a dairy cow and would very much like to sell me milk from said cow (unless, of course, he is willing to spend thousands of dollars to pasteurize the milk and comply with a bevy of other federal and state regulations.)[63]

However, not only is it illegal for me to purchase milk from my neighbor the farmer, as the following case demonstrates, the price I pay for milk at the grocery store is also largely controlled by the civil magistrate. As you read the case, consider how greatly economic liberty and the concomitant freedom of contract has been eroded in the past century or so.

Hettinga v. United States
677 F.3d 471 (D.C. Cir. 2012)

PER CURIAM:

Plaintiff-appellants Hein and Ellen Hettinga appeal the dismissal of their constitutional challenges to two provisions of the Milk Regulatory Equity Act of 2005 ("MREA"). The Hettingas alleged that the provisions, which subjected certain large producer-handlers of milk to contribution requirements applicable to all milk handlers, constituted a bill of attainder and violated the Equal Protection and Due Process Clauses. The district court disagreed, and we affirm.

---

[62] *National Federation of Independent Businesses v. Sebelius,* ___ U.S. ___, 132 S.Ct. 2566 (2012) (upholding Obamacare as Constitutional in a very split and arguably irrational opinion).

[63] *See, e.g.,* Joel Salatin, *Everything I Want to do is Illegal: War Stories from the Local Food Front* 12-26 (2007) and Ron Schmid, *The Untold Story of Milk: the History, Politics, and Science of Nature's Perfect Food: Raw Milk from Pasture-Fed Cows* (2005).

I

Milk markets in the United States are regulated by a complex system of price controls dating back to the New Deal. The Agricultural Marketing Agreement Act of 1937, ("AMAA"), authorizes the Secretary of Agriculture to issue regional milk marketing orders that govern payments from milk processors and distributors ("handlers") to dairy farmers ("producers"). *Id.* Under a typical milk market order, a dairy farmer supplies raw milk to a processor or distributor, and the handler pays money into a centralized "producer settlement fund" at fixed prices based on the intended use of the milk. Handlers using their milk for "high value" uses, such as fluid milk, pay higher prices than handlers that engage in "low-value" uses, such as the processing of butter or cheese. The money that handlers pay into the producer settlement fund is then proportionally redistributed to milk producers at a uniform "blend price" based on quantity of milk sold. This system ensures that all dairy farmers receive the same price for their raw milk regardless of whether they sell to high-value or low-value handlers.

Firms that operate as both producers and handlers create serious complications for this system. In such cases, there is no opportunity for the producer-handler to pay into the centralized producer settlement fund because there is no intermediate sale of raw milk. Until recently, the Secretary of Agriculture therefore exempted producer-handlers from the pricing and pooling requirements of federal milk marketing orders. The pricing and pooling requirements also did not apply to handlers who sold milk in geographic areas that were not regulated by federal milk marketing orders, even if the handler itself was located in a federally-regulated area.

The Hettingas own two dairy operations that fell within these exemptions. The first is Sarah Farms, an integrated producer-handler located in Yuma, Arizona. Sarah Farms processes and sells over three million pounds of its own milk per month in the federally regulated Arizona Marketing Area. The second is GH Dairy, an independent milk processing plant which they own in partnership with their son. GH Dairy, a handler located in Arizona, processes raw milk into bottled milk and milk products that are sold exclusively in California. Because California is not a federally regulated milk marketing area, GH Dairy was not subject to the federal pricing and pooling requirements.

On February 24, 2006, the USDA adopted a Final Rule that would have eliminated the producer-handler exemption for firms that operate in the Arizona and Pacific Northwest Marketing Areas and sell more than three million pounds of their own milk per month—a group that includes Sarah Farms. *See Milk in the Pacific Northwest and Arizona–Las Vegas Marketing Areas; Order Amending the Orders,* 71 Fed.Reg. 9,430 (Feb. 24, 2006) ("USDA Rule"). The decision to eliminate the exemption for these large producer-handlers was based on evidence of "disorderly marketing conditions"— specifically, that large producer-handlers were obtaining a "competitive sales advantage" over fully-regulated handlers, and were causing a "measurabl[e] and significant[ ]" decrease in the blend price being paid to regulated producers. *Milk in the Pacific Northwest and Arizona–Las Vegas Marketing Areas; Final Decision on Proposed Amendments to Marketing Agreement and to Orders,* 70 Fed.Reg. 74,166, 74,186–88 (Dec. 14, 2005). The USDA Rule was scheduled to go into effect on April 1, 2006. The Hettingas filed suit in the U.S. District Court for the Northern District of Texas, challenging the legality of the USDA Rule and seeking a preliminary injunction Oral argument was scheduled for March 29, 2006.

On the day before the Texas district court heard arguments in the Hettingas' case, Congress amended the AMAA by passing the MREA. President Bush subsequently signed the MREA into law on April 11, 2006. Subsection N of the MREA, 7 U.S.C. § 608c(5)(N), codified the USDA Rule's revocation of the exemption for large producer-handlers in the Arizona Marketing Area, including Sarah Farms. Unlike the USDA Rule, however, it applied neither to Nevada, which Congress exempted from coverage by any federal milk marketing orders, nor to the Pacific Northwest Milk Marketing Area. Subsection M of the MREA, *id.* § 608c(5)(M), imposed the federal pricing and pooling requirements on handlers, like GH Dairy, that were located in a federally regulated area but sold packaged milk exclusively in a state not covered by a federal milk marketing order, such as California.

The Hettingas challenged the constitutionality of the MREA in the U.S. District Court for the District of Columbia. First, they alleged that Subsections M and N of the MREA violate the Bill of Attainder Clause by singling them out for legislative punishment. Compl. ¶¶ 53–57. Second, the Hettingas claim the MREA denies them equal protection by "singling them out for adverse treatment that is extended to no other producer-handler in any other Milk Marketing Area." *Id.* ¶ 65. Finally, they claim the MREA denied them due process of law by foreclosing judicial review of the USDA Rule in the Northern District of Texas. *Id.* ¶ 60. The district court initially dismissed the Hettingas' claims for failure to exhaust administrative remedies, but this Court reversed and remanded, holding that the AMAA's exhaustion requirements do not apply to facial constitutional challenges. *Hettinga v. United States,* 560 F.3d 498, 504–06 (D.C.Cir.2009). On remand, the district court dismissed the Hettingas' complaint for failure to state a claim under Fed.R.Civ.P. 12(b)(6) and denied leave to file a supplemental complaint. *Hettinga v. United States,* 770 F.Supp.2d 51 (D.D.C.2011).

. . .

II

[In this section of the opinion, based upon prior Supreme Court precedent, the court denied the Hettingas' argument that the MREA amounts to a bill of attainder because it applies only to them.]

III

We grant statutes involving economic policy a "strong presumption of validity." *FCC v. Beach Commc'ns, Inc.*, 508 U.S. 307, 314, 113 S.Ct. 2096, 124 L.Ed.2d 211 (1993). A statutory classification that "neither proceeds along suspect lines nor infringes fundamental constitutional rights must be upheld against equal protection challenge if there is any reasonably conceivable state of facts that could provide a rational basis for the classification." *Id.* at 313, 113 S.Ct. 2096. "Where there are plausible reasons for Congress' action, our inquiry is at an end." *Id.* at 313–14, 113 S.Ct. 2096. The challenger bears the burden of showing that the statute is not a rational means of advancing a legitimate government purpose. *See Bd. of Trs. of the Univ. of Ala. v. Garrett*, 531 U.S. 356, 367, 121 S.Ct. 955, 148 L.Ed.2d 866 (2001).

The district court dismissed the Hettingas' equal protection claim because it found the MREA provides a rational means of ensuring orderly milk markets by (1) preventing handlers located in regulated regions from gaining advantages over their competitors by exporting milk to unregulated regions and (2) preventing large producer-handlers in a federally-regulated region from undercutting other handlers in that region with unregulated sales. On appeal, the Hettingas claim the district court applied too deferential a standard of review, arguing that rational basis review is "not [ ] toothless." *Logan v. Zimmerman Brush Co.*, 455 U.S. 422, 439, 102 S.Ct. 1148, 71 L.Ed.2d 265 (1982) (Blackmun, J., concurring).

Regardless of how Justice Blackmun characterized rational basis review, the Supreme Court's subsequent decision in *Beach* makes clear that "not toothless" does not mean "growling." Here, the government provided a rational explanation for its decision to close two loopholes in the AMAA scheme—that large dairy businesses have used the exemptions to gain a substantial—and ultimately disruptive—competitive advantage over their regulated competitors. *Beach* requires us to accept this explanation and end our inquiry here. *See Beach Commc'ns*, 508 U.S. at 313–14, 113 S.Ct. 2096. Although the classification might indeed be unfair to the Hettingas, mere disparity of treatment is not sufficient to state an equal protection violation.

. . .

For the foregoing reasons, the decision of the district court is

Affirmed.

BROWN, Circuit Judge, with whom Chief Judge SENTELLE joins, concurring:

I agree fully with the court's opinion. Given the long-standing precedents in this area no other result is possible. Our precedents forced the

Hettingas to make a difficult legal argument. No doubt they would have preferred a simpler one—that the operation and production of their enterprises had been impermissibly collectivized—but a long line of constitutional adjudication precluded that claim.

The Hettingas' sense of ill-usage is understandable. So is their consternation at being confronted with the gap between the rhetoric of free markets and the reality of ubiquitous regulation. The Hettingas' collision with the MREA—the latest iteration of the venerable AMAA—reveals an ugly truth: America's cowboy capitalism was long ago disarmed by a democratic process increasingly dominated by powerful groups with economic interests antithetical to competitors and consumers. And the courts, from which the victims of burdensome regulation sought protection, have been negotiating the terms of surrender since the 1930s.

First the Supreme Court allowed state and local jurisdictions to regulate property, pursuant to their police powers, in the public interest, and to "adopt whatever economic policy may reasonably be deemed to promote public welfare." *Nebbia v. New York*, 291 U.S. 502, 516, 54 S.Ct. 505, 78 L.Ed. 940 (1934). Then the Court relegated economic liberty to a lower echelon of constitutional protection than personal or political liberty, according restrictions on property rights only minimal review. *United States v. Carolene Products Co.*, 304 U.S. 144, 152–53, 58 S.Ct. 778, 82 L.Ed. 1234 (1938). Finally, the Court abdicated its constitutional duty to protect economic rights completely, acknowledging that the only recourse for aggrieved property owners lies in the "democratic process." *Vance v. Bradley*, 440 U.S. 93, 97, 99 S.Ct. 939, 59 L.Ed.2d 171 (1979). "The Constitution," the Court said, "presumes that, absent some reason to infer antipathy, even improvident decisions will eventually be rectified by the democratic process and that judicial intervention is generally unwarranted no matter how unwisely we may think a political branch has acted." *Id.*

As the dissent predicted in *Nebbia*, the judiciary's refusal to consider the wisdom of legislative acts—at least to inquire whether its purpose and the means proposed are "within legislative power"—would lead to only one result: "[R]ights guaranteed by the Constitution [would] exist only so long as supposed public interest does not require their extinction." 291 U.S. at 523, 54 S.Ct. 505. In short order that baleful prophecy received the court's imprimatur. In *Carolene Products* (yet another case involving protectionist legislation), the court ratified minimalist review of economic regulations, holding that a rational basis for economic legislation would be presumed and more searching inquiry would be reserved for intrusions on political rights. 304 U.S. at 153 n. 4, 58 S.Ct. 778.

Thus the Supreme Court decided economic liberty was not a fundamental constitutional right, and decreed economic legislation must be upheld against an equal protection challenge "if there is any reasonably conceivable state of facts that could provide a rational basis" for it. *FCC v. Beach Commc'ns, Inc.*, 508 U.S. 307, 313, 113 S.Ct. 2096, 124 L.Ed.2d 211 (1993). *See also Pac. States Box & Basket Co. v. White*, 296 U.S. 176, 185–86,

56 S.Ct. 159, 80 L.Ed. 138 (1935); *Steffan v. Perry,* 41 F.3d 677, 684–85 (D.C.Cir.1994) (en banc).

This standard is particularly troubling in light of the pessimistic view of human nature that animated the Framing of the Constitution—a worldview that the American polity and its political handmaidens have, unfortunately, shown to be largely justified. *See* James Madison, *Notes of Debates in the Federal Convention of 1787,* at 39, 42 (W.W. Norton & Co. 1987). Moreover, what the Framers theorized about the destructive potential of factions (now known as special or group interests), experience has also shown to be true. The Federalist No. 10, at 78, 81 (James Madison) (Clinton Rossiter ed., 1961). The judiciary has worried incessantly about the "countermajoritarian difficulty" when interpreting the Constitution. But the better view may be that the Constitution *created* the countermajoritarian difficulty in order to thwart more potent threats to the Republic: the political temptation to exploit the public appetite for other people's money—either by buying consent with broad-based entitlements or selling subsidies, licensing restrictions, tariffs, or price fixing regimes to benefit narrow special interests.

The Hettingas believe they are the victims of just such shenanigans. Compl. ¶¶ 40–45. And press accounts during the height of the controversy support the claim. *See* Dan Morgan, Sarah Cohen, & Gilbert M. Gaul, "Dairy Industry Crushed Innovator Who Bested Price–Control System," Wash. Post, Dec. 10, 2006, *available at* http://www.washingtonpost.com/wpdyn/content/article/2006/12/09/AR200612 0900925.html. The Washington Post described Hein Hettinga as an American success story. He emigrated to the U.S. after World War II and started as a hired hand. By 1990, Hettinga owned half a dozen dairies and decided to build his own bottling business. A Costco vice president showed reporters copies of an e-mail he sent to Senator Reid during the legislative debate, explaining that Southern California purchasers of milk were the victims of "a brazen case of price gouging and profiteering by the strongest, largest market suppliers," who turned a deaf ear to the company's call for lower prices. Hein Hettinga changed all that. His arrangement with Costco "lowered the average price of milk by 20 cents a gallon overnight" until two senators, one from each party, pushed through the milk legislation at issue in this case.

Very little seems to have changed since the Supreme Court's initial confrontation with the regulation of milk pricing in *Nebbia.* The state of New York, responding to falling prices caused by the Great Depression, created a Milk Control Board, which proposed to remedy weak demand by establishing a minimum price for milk, and making sale of milk at any lower price a crime. 291 U.S. at 515, 519, 54 S.Ct. 505. Leo Nebbia sold two quarts of milk and a five-cent loaf of bread for eighteen cents, and was convicted of violating the board's order. *Id.* at 515, 54 S.Ct. 505.

Even Justice McReynolds saw the irony. The law, he said, "impose[d] direct and arbitrary burdens upon those already seriously impoverished" to give special benefits to others. *Id.* at 557, 54 S.Ct. 505. "To him with less than

9 cents it says: You cannot procure a quart of milk from the grocer although he is anxious to accept what you can pay and the demands of your household are urgent! A superabundance; but no child can purchase from a willing storekeeper below the figure appointed by three men at headquarters!" *Id.* at 557–58, 54 S.Ct. 505.

To be sure, the economic climate in which the New York legislature enacted the law at issue in *Nebbia* was truly dire, but 78 years later, the same tired trope about "disorderly market conduct" is still extant. The Hettingas built their business on an exemption—one that was profitable for them and beneficial for consumers. The government acknowledged that the decision to eliminate the exemption was based on evidence that large producer-handlers were obtaining a "decisive competitive advantage" over fully-regulated handlers, Appellees' Br. at 7, and were causing a measurable and "significant[ ]" decrease in the blend prices being paid to regulated handlers. *See* 70 Fed.Reg. 74,166, 74,186 (Dec. 14, 2005). As another court has noted, federal regulation of milk pricing "is premised on dissatisfaction with the results of competition." *Alto Dairy v. Veneman,* 336 F.3d 560, 562 (7th Cir.2003). "[M]ilk price discrimination is intended to redistribute wealth from consumers to producers of milk." *Id.* Once again, the government has thwarted the free market, and ultimately hurt consumers, to protect the economic interests of a powerful faction. Neither the legislators nor the lobbyists broke any positive laws to accomplish this result. It just *seems* like a crime.

The judiciary justifies its reluctance to intervene by claiming incompetence—apparently, judges lack the acumen to recognize corruption, self-interest, or arbitrariness in the economic realm—or deferring to the majoritarian imperative. *But see* The Federalist No. 78, at 467 (Alexander Hamilton) (Clinton Rossiter ed., 1961). The practical effect of rational basis review of economic regulation is the absence of any check on the group interests that all too often control the democratic process. It allows the legislature free rein to subjugate the common good and individual liberty to the electoral calculus of politicians, the whim of majorities, or the self-interest of factions. *See* Randy E. Barnett, Restoring the Lost Constitution: The Presumption of Liberty 260 (2004).

The hope of correction at the ballot box is purely illusory. *See generally* Ilya Somin, *Political Ignorance and the Counter–Majoritarian Difficulty: A New Perspective on the Central Obsession of Constitutional Theory,* 89 Iowa L.Rev. 1287 (2004). In an earlier century, H.L. Mencken offered a blunt assessment of that option: "[G]overnment is a broker in pillage, and every election is a sort of advance auction sale of stolen goods." On Politics: A Carnival of Buncombe 331 (1996). And, as the Hettingas can attest, it's no good hoping the process will heal itself. Civil society, "once it grows addicted to redistribution, changes its character and comes to require the state to 'feed its habit.'" Anthony De Jasay, The State 226 (1998). The difficulty of assessing net benefits and burdens makes the idea of public choice oxymoronic. *See id.* at 248. Rational basis review means property is at the mercy of the pillagers. The constitutional guarantee of liberty deserves more respect—a lot more.

GRIFFITH, Circuit Judge, concurring:

I, too, agree fully with the per curiam opinion, but do not join my colleagues' concurrence with its spirited criticism of the Supreme Court's long-standing approach to claims of economic liberty. Although by no means unsympathetic to their criticism nor critical of their choice to express their perspective, I am reluctant to set forth my own views on the wisdom of such a broad area of the Supreme Court's settled jurisprudence that was not challenged by the petitioner.

Notes and Questions

1. Got Milk? As this case demonstrates, there is much more behind buying that gallon of milk at the grocery store than most of us realize. Prior to reading this, did you know the extent of the regulations and control on the milk industry in America? Does it surprise you? Do you think most Americans know and understand all of this? (And, of course, milk is just one example. Many other areas of the economy, from employment relationships to other agricultural products to airlines to securities, are heavily regulated with the government dictating many, if not most, of the terms of the contracts in these areas.)

Is there something unjust about the very fact alone that this is all so complicated and secret? Obviously, it can be found out, but, while the milk industry very much wants you to ask the question "Got milk?", they do not want you to consider how you got it.

2. The Erosion of Economic Liberty. Can you explain how regulations and controls, such as those described in this case, erode our economic liberty? In explaining this, perhaps it would help you to consider some additional questions.

Who benefits from regulations and controls such as these? Consumers? Producers? Farmers? Big companies or small companies or family farms? Review the dissenting opinion above. What do the dissenting judges think?

What is the proper role of the government here? Do these regulations and controls fit within punishing evildoers? Or, do they simply work to transfer wealth from one group to another as the dissent suggests? If so, where does transferring wealth fit within the biblical role of the civil magistrate described previously? What would a Christian worldview answer look like? How would Judge Posner answer this issue?

How do you think such as system is justified to the public when it is discussed? Are you persuaded by these justifications?

Do these regulations make it easier or harder for competitors to enter the milk market? If you felt called to go into small-scale, natural dairy farming, would these regulations make it harder or easier for you to do that?

Why should the government dictate the terms of the contracts that you would enter into if you want to sell the milk and your neighbors want to buy it?

3. The Most Lenient Standard of Review. The Supreme Court uses different tests in reviewing government actions to consider whether they violate rights guaranteed by the Constitution. Some of these tests are very, very demanding, and very few laws survive analysis under these tests (for example, strict scrutiny analysis.) However, for economic liberty issues, the Supreme Court has adopted the most lenient standard of review—rational basis. This reflects a view that economic liberty is not as important as other types of liberty. Do you agree with the Supreme Court? Or, are you persuaded by the dissenting opinion in *Hettinga*? With whom do you think Judge Posner would side?

The following materials were chosen to introduce you to tort law from a Christian perspective and to provide you with a famous case representing a modern, law-and-economics view of tort law. First, you will read a selection of verses from *The Bible* representing its teachings on tort law. Second, you will read an old case (1400s) from England dealing with torts. Finally, you will read *United States v. Carroll Towing Co.*, one of the most famous tort cases of all time.

As you read these materials, consider the following questions: What should the purpose of tort law be? What does it appear to be under the biblical system? What about the older common law represented by *The Case of the Thorns*? What about the law and economics view? What should the proper tort law system be: negligence or strict liability? Which is more consistent with *The Bible*? The common law? Law and economics?

Exodus 21:18-19, 22-36; 22:5-6
English Standard Version

---

[18] "When men quarrel and one strikes the other with a stone or with his fist and the man does not die but takes to his bed, [19] then if the man rises again and walks outdoors with his staff, he who struck him shall be clear; only he shall pay for the loss of his time, and shall have him thoroughly healed.
   * * *

[22] "When men strive together and hit a pregnant woman, so that her children come out, but there is no harm, the one who hit her shall surely be fined, as the woman's husband shall impose on him, and he shall pay as the judges determine. [23] But if there is harm, then you shall pay life for life, [24] eye for eye, tooth for tooth, hand for hand, foot for foot, [25] burn for burn, wound for wound, stripe for stripe.

[26] "When a man strikes the eye of his slave, male or female, and destroys it, he shall let the slave go free because of his eye. [27] If he knocks out the tooth of his slave, male or female, he shall let the slave go free because of his tooth.

[28] "When an ox gores a man or a woman to death, the ox shall be stoned, and its flesh shall not be eaten, but the owner of the ox shall not be liable. [29] But if the ox has been accustomed to gore in the past, and its owner has been warned but has not kept it in, and it kills a man or a woman, the ox shall be stoned, and its owner also shall be put to death. [30] If a ransom is imposed on him, then he shall give for the redemption of his life whatever is imposed on him. [31] If it gores a man's son or daughter, he shall be dealt with according to this same rule. [32] If the ox gores a slave, male or female, the owner shall give to their master thirty shekels of silver, and the ox shall be stoned.

[33] "When a man opens a pit, or when a man digs a pit and does not cover it, and an ox or a donkey falls into it, [34] the owner of the pit shall make restoration. He shall give money to its owner, and the dead beast shall be his.

[35] "When one man's ox butts another's, so that it dies, then they shall sell the live ox and share its price, and the dead beast also they shall share. [36] Or if it is known that the ox has been accustomed to gore in the past, and its owner has not kept it in, he shall repay ox for ox, and the dead beast shall be his.

* * *

[5] "If a man causes a field or vineyard to be grazed over, or lets his beast loose and it feeds in another man's field, he shall make restitution from the best in his own field and in his own vineyard.

[6] "If fire breaks out and catches in thorns so that the stacked grain or the standing grain or the field is consumed, he who started the fire shall make full restitution.

The Case of the Thorns (Hull v. Orange)
Y.B. Mich. 6 Edw. 4, fo. 7, pl. 18 (K.B. 1466)[64]

Trespass *quare vi & armis clausum fregit, & herbam suam pedibus conculcando consumpsit*[65] in six acres. The defendant pleads, that he hath an acre lying next the said six acres, and upon it a hedge of thorns, and he cut the thorns, and they *ipso invito* fell upon the plaintiff's land, and the defendant took them off as soon as he could, which is the same trespass; and the plaintiff demurred; and adjudged for the plaintiff; for though a man doth a lawful thing, yet if any damage do thereby befal another, he shall answer for it, if he could have avoided it. As if a man lop a tree, and the boughs fall upon another *ipso invito*, yet an action lies. If a man shoot at buts, and hurt another unawares, an action lies. I have land through which a river runs to your mill, and I lop

---

[64] This case is a very early English tort case, which has been preserved in various texts in a variety of forms. The version used here is from a summary of the case found in *Bessey v. Olliot & Lambert*, Raym. Sir T. 467-468 (K.B. 1681). Of *The Case of the Thorns*, the Court wrote: "In all civil acts the law doth not so much regard the intent of the actor, as the loss and damage of the party suffering."

[65] Editor's Note: Meaning that the vegetation was damaged.

the fallows growing upon the river side, which accidentally stop the water, so as your mill is hindered, an action lies. If I am building my own house, and a piece of timber falls on my neighbour's house and breaks part of it, an action lies. If a man assault me, and I lift up my staff to defend myself, and in lifting it up hit another, an action lies by that person, and yet I did a lawful thing. And the reason of all these cases is, because he that is damaged ought to be recompensed. But otherwise it is in criminal cases, for there *actus non facit reuni nisi mens sit rea*.[66]

United States v. Carroll Towing Co.
159 F.2d 169 (2d Cir. 1947)

L. HAND, Circuit Judge.

[This case involved the sinking of a barge, the "Anna C," on January 4, 1944, in the North River in New York Harbor. Multiple companies were involved and multiple claims leveled by the various parties against one another. The Connors Marine Co., Inc., was the owner of the barge, and the Pennsylvania Railroad Company had chartered the barge. Through the actions of a number of parties in a busy part of New York Harbor, the "Anna C" eventually sank causing the loss of her cargo, among other things. One of the issues involved whether "the absence of a bargee or other attendant will make the owner of the barge liable for injuries to other vessels if she breaks away from her moorings."]

It appears from the foregoing review that there is no general rule to determine when the absence of a bargee or other attendant will make the owner of the barge liable for injuries to other vessels if she breaks away from her moorings. However, in any cases where he would be so liable for injuries to others obviously he must reduce his damages proportionately, if the injury is to his own barge. It becomes apparent why there can be no such general rule, when we consider the grounds for such a liability. Since there are occasions when every vessel will break from her moorings, and since, if she does, she becomes a menace to those about her; the owner's duty, as in other similar situations, to provide against resulting injuries is a function of three variables: (1) The probability that she will break away; (2) the gravity of the resulting injury, if she does; (3) the burden of adequate precautions. Possibly it serves to bring this notion into relief to state it in algebraic terms: if the probability be called P; the injury, L; and the burden, B; liability depends upon whether B is less than L multiplied by P: i.e., whether $B < PL$. Applied to the situation at bar, the likelihood that a barge will break from her fasts and the damage she will do, vary with the place and time; for example, if a storm

---

[66] Editor's Note: Meaning that in criminal law both a guilty state of mind as well as a guilty act is required.

threatens, the danger is greater; so it is, if she is in a crowded harbor where moored barges are constantly being shifted about. On the other hand, the barge must not be the bargee's prison, even though he lives aboard; he must go ashore at times. We need not say whether, even in such crowded waters as New York Harbor a bargee must be aboard at night at all; it may be that the custom is otherwise, . . . and that, if so, the situation is one where custom should control. We leave that question open; but we hold that it is not in all cases a sufficient answer to a bargee's absence without excuse, during working hours, that he has properly made fast his barge to a pier, when he leaves her. In the case at bar the bargee left at five o'clock in the afternoon of January 3rd, and the flotilla broke away at about two o'clock in the afternoon of the following day, twenty-one hours afterwards. The bargee had been away all the time, and we hold that his fabricated story was affirmative evidence that he had no excuse for his absence. At the *locus in quo*—especially during the short January days and in the full tide of war activity—barges were being constantly 'drilled' in and out. Certainly it was not beyond reasonable expectation that, with the inevitable haste and bustle, the work might not be done with adequate care. In such circumstances we hold—and it is all that we do hold—that it was a fair requirement that the Conners Company should have a bargee aboard (unless he had some excuse for his absence), during the working hours of daylight.

Notes and Questions

1. Purpose of Tort Law? After reading and reflecting upon the foregoing, what should the purpose of tort law be? Should it be to compensate the injured? Or, should it be the prevention and reduction of accidents?

The biblical law seems to be far more concerned with the compensation of the injured, as was the older common law cases, such as *The Case of the Thorns*, which tended to impose strict liability for injuries caused. Law and economics, on the hand, represented above by the *Carroll Towing Co.* case, is focused instead upon setting legal rules and standards designed to prevent or reduce accidents in the future. Which do you find more compelling as the proper purpose for tort law?

Lastly, consider how this purpose is determined. The older common law cases use a law of nature and nature's God approach. In the higher law, in this case, *The Bible*, a purpose to compensate those injured is recognized or discovered. The law and economics approach, rejecting any notion of higher law, looks instead to the maximization of society's wealth. Society's wealth is maximized by the efficient prevention of accidents. Remember, law and economics is not concerned with individual winners and losers, but rather society as a whole. It is of no moment how the parties before the court are affected personally, but rather the concern is how the standard set and the resolution of the case will impact future behavior of many, many parties and thereby society as a whole.

2. Judicial v. Prudential Reasoning Revisited. As previously stated, the three issues for analysis in the Christian worldview of law arise in all areas of law. Which of the above approaches to tort law is more consistent with judicial reasoning? How about prudential reasoning?

The biblical law and the older common law approach lends itself nicely to judicial style reasoning. There is a set standard of conduct, and the court looks at the facts of the case (backward-looking), determines whether the facts of the case meet or fall short of the standard, and based upon that determination decides liability.

The law and economics approach is instead focused upon setting the proper rule or standard that will minimize accidents in the future. While the Learned Hand formula does serve as a standard for past conduct, the purpose of its formulation is not primarily to compensate those injured by past conduct. Rather, it is designed to set a standard that will result in the optimal level of precautions v. accidents in the future. Accordingly, Judge Learned Hand, in stating the standard, is engaged in prudential reasoning. He is looking forward and asking "What is an efficient standard for tort liability?"

3. Strict Liability or Negligence? Answers to the above questions end up having a very real impact on even the standard used to impose liability. While it is a question of some debate, many would argue that the biblical system is primarily a system of strict liability. Certainly the older common law standard was one of strict liability.[67] Law and economics and modern tort law, as demonstrated by *Carroll Towing Co.*, is dominated by the negligence standard.

After reading the above materials and Judge Posner's tort materials, what do you think? Should the standard be one of strict liability or of negligence? How did you decide?

---

[67] *See, e.g.,* Douglas H. Cook, *Negligence or Strict Liability? A Study in Biblical Tort Law,* 13 Whittier L. Rev. 1 (1992) and Titus, *God, Man, and Law* 161-165 (1994).

The Queen v. Dudley and Stephens
14 Q.B.D. 273 (1884)

* * *

INDICTMENT for the murder of Richard Parker on the high seas within the jurisdiction of the Admiralty.

At the trial before Huddleston, B., at the Devon and Cornwall Winter Assizes, November 7, 1884, the jury, at the suggestion of the learned judge, found the facts of the case in a special verdict which stated "that on July 5, 1884, the prisoners, Thomas Dudley and Edward Stephens, with one Brooks, all able-bodied English seamen, and the deceased also an English boy, between seventeen and eighteen years of age, the crew of an English yacht, a registered English vessel, were cast away in a storm on the high seas 1600 miles from the Cape of Good Hope, and were compelled to put into an open boat belonging to the said yacht. That in this boat they had no supply of water and no supply of food, except two 1 lb. tins of turnips, and for three days they had nothing else to subsist upon. That on the fourth day they caught a small turtle, upon which they subsisted for a few days, and this was the only food they had up to the twentieth day when the act now in question was committed. That on the twelfth day the remains of the turtle were entirely consumed, and for the next eight days they had nothing to eat. That they had no fresh water, except such rain as they from time to time caught in their oilskin capes. That the boat was drifting on the ocean, and was probably more than 1000 miles away from land. That on the eighteenth day, when they had been seven days without food and five without water, the prisoners spoke to Brooks as to what should be done if no succour came, and suggested that someone should be sacrificed to save the rest, but Brooks dissented, and the boy, to whom they were understood to refer, was not consulted. That on the 24th of July, the day before the act now in question, the prisoner Dudley proposed to Stephens and Brooks that lots should be cast who should be put to death to save the rest, but Brooks refused to consent, and it was not put to the boy, and in point of fact there was no drawing of lots. That on that day the prisoners spoke of their having families, and suggested it would be better to kill the boy that their lives should be saved, and Dudley proposed that if there was no vessel in sight by the morrow morning the boy should be killed. That next day, the 25th of July, no vessel appearing, Dudley told Brooks that he had better go and have a sleep, and made signs to Stephens and Brooks that the boy had better be killed. The prisoner Stephens agreed to the act, but Brooks dissented from it. That the boy was then lying at the bottom of the boat quite helpless, and extremely weakened by famine and by drinking sea water, and unable to make any resistance, nor did he ever assent to his being killed. The prisoner Dudley offered a prayer asking forgiveness for them all if either of them should be tempted to commit a rash act, and that their souls might be saved. That Dudley, with the assent of Stephens, went to the boy, and telling him that his time was come, put a knife into his throat and killed him then and there; that the three men fed upon the body and blood of the boy for four days; that on the fourth day after the act had been committed the boat was picked up by a passing vessel, and the prisoners were rescued, still alive, but in the lowest state of prostration. That they were carried to the port of Falmouth, and committed for trial at Exeter. That if the men had not fed upon the body of the boy they would probably not have survived to be so picked up and rescued, but would within the four days have died of famine. That the boy, being in a much weaker condition, was likely to have died before them. That at the time of the act in question there was no sail in sight, nor any reasonable prospect of relief. That under these circumstances there appeared to the prisoners every probability that unless they then fed or very soon fed upon the boy or one of themselves they would die of starvation. That there was no appreciable chance of saving life except by killing someone for the others to eat. That assuming any necessity to kill anybody, there was no greater necessity for killing the boy than any of the other three men." But whether upon the whole matter by the jurors found the killing of Richard Parker by Dudley and Stephens be felony and murder the jurors are ignorant, and pray the advice of the Court thereupon, and if upon the whole matter the Court shall be of opinion that the killing of Richard Parker be felony and murder, then the jurors say that Dudley and Stephens were each guilty of felony and murder as alleged in the indictment."

The learned judge then adjourned the assizes until the 25th of November at the Royal Courts of Justice. . . .

* * *

LORD COLERIDGE, C.J.

The two prisoners, Thomas Dudley and Edwin Stephens, were indicted for the murder of Richard Parker on the high seas on the 25th of July in the present year. They were tried before my Brother Huddleston at Exeter on the 6th of November, and, under the direction of my learned Brother, the jury returned a special verdict, the legal effect of which has been argued before us, and on which we are now to pronounce judgment.

The special verdict as, after certain objections by Mr. Collins to which the Attorney General yielded, it is finally settled before us is as follows. [His

Lordship read the special verdict as above set out.] From these facts, stated with the cold precision of a special verdict, it appears sufficiently that the prisoners were subject to terrible temptation, to sufferings which might break down the bodily power of the strongest man, and try the conscience of the best. Other details yet more harrowing, facts still more loathsome and appalling, were presented to the jury, and are to be found recorded in my learned Brother's notes. But nevertheless this is clear, that the prisoners put to death a weak and unoffending boy upon the chance of preserving their own lives by feeding upon his flesh and blood after he was killed, and with the certainty of depriving *him* of any possible chance of survival. The verdict finds in terms that "if the men had not fed upon the body of the boy they would *probably* not have survived," and that "the boy being in a much weaker condition was *likely* to have died before them." They might possibly have been picked up next day by a passing ship; they might possibly not have been picked up at all; in either case it is obvious that the killing of the boy would have been an unnecessary and profitless act. It is found by the verdict that the boy was incapable of resistance, and, in fact, made none; and it is not even suggested that his death was due to any violence on his part attempted against, or even so much as feared by, those who killed him. Under these circumstances the jury say that they are ignorant whether those who killed him were guilty of murder, and have referred it to this Court to determine what is the legal consequence which follows from the facts which they have found.

     * * *

[The Court first dealt with some procedural objections before moving to "the real question in the case."]

There remains to be considered the real question in the case—whether killing under the circumstances set forth in the verdict be or be not murder. The contention that it could be anything else was, to the minds of us all, both new and strange, and we stopped the Attorney General in his negative argument in order that we might hear what could be said in support of a proposition which appeared to us to be at once dangerous, immoral, and opposed to all legal principle and analogy. All, no doubt, that can be said has been urged before us, and we are now to consider and determine what it amounts to. First it is said that it follows from various definitions of murder in books of authority, which definitions imply, if they do not state, the doctrine, that in order to save your own life you may lawfully take away the life of another, when that other is neither attempting nor threatening yours, nor is guilty of any illegal act whatever towards you or anyone else. But if these definitions be looked at they will not be found to sustain this contention. The earliest in point of date is the passage cited to us from Bracton, who lived in the reign of Henry III. It was at one time the fashion to discredit Bracton, as Mr. Reeve tells us, because he was supposed to mingle too much of the canonist and civilian with the common lawyer. There is now no such feeling, but the passage upon homicide, on which reliance is placed, is a remarkable example of the kind of writing which may explain it. Sin and crime are spoken of as apparently equally illegal, and the crime of murder, it is expressly declared, may be committed "*linguâ vel facto*"; so that a man, like Hero "done to death by slanderous tongues," would, it seems, in the opinion of Bracton, be a person in respect of whom might be grounded a legal indictment for murder. But in the very passage as to necessity, on which reliance has been placed, it is clear that Bracton is speaking of necessity in the ordinary sense—the repelling by violence, violence justified so far as it was necessary for the object, any illegal violence used towards oneself. If, says Bracton, the necessity be "*evitabilis, et evadere posset absque occisione, tunc erit reus homicidii*"—words which shew clearly that he is thinking of physical danger from which *escape* may be possible, and that the "*inevitabilis necessitas*" of which he speaks as justifying homicide is a necessity of the same nature.

It is, if possible, yet clearer that the doctrine contended for receives no support from the great authority of Lord Hale. It is plain that in his view the necessity which justified homicide is that only which has always been and is now considered a justification. "In all these cases of homicide by necessity," says he, "as in pursuit of a felon, in killing him that assaults to rob, or comes to burn or break a house, or the like, which are in themselves no felony" (1 Hale's Pleas of the Crown, p. 491). Again, he says that "the necessity which justifies homicide is of two kinds: (1) the necessity which is of a private nature; (2) the necessity which relates to the public justice and safety. The former is that necessity which obligeth a man to his own defence and safeguard, and this takes in these inquiries:—(1.) What may be done for the safeguard of a man's own life;" and then follow three other heads not necessary to pursue. Then Lord Hale proceeds:—"As touching the first of these—viz., homicide in defence of a man's own life, which is usually styled *se defendendo*." It is not possible to use words more clear to shew that Lord Hale regarded the private necessity which justified, and alone justified, the taking the life of another for the safeguard of one's own to be what is commonly called "self-defence." (Hale's Pleas of the Crown, i. 478.)

But if this could be even doubtful upon Lord Hale's words, Lord Hale himself has made it clear. For in the chapter in which he deals with the exemption created by compulsion or necessity he thus expresses himself:— "If a man be desperately assaulted and in peril of death, and cannot otherwise escape unless, to satisfy his assailant's fury, he will kill an innocent person then present, the fear and actual force will not acquit him of the crime and punishment of murder, if he commit the fact, for he ought rather to die himself than kill an innocent; but if he cannot otherwise save his own life the law permits him in his own defence to kill the assailant, for by the violence of the assault, and the offence committed upon him by the assailant himself, the law of nature, and necessity, hath made him his own protector *cum debito moderamine inculpatœ tutelœ*." (Hale's Pleas of the Crown, vol. i. 51.)

But, further still, Lord Hale in the following chapter deals with the position asserted by the casuists, and sanctioned, as he says, by Grotius and Puffendorf, that in a case of extreme necessity, either of hunger or clothing; "theft is no theft, or at least not punishable as theft, as some even of our own lawyers have asserted the same." "But," says Lord Hale, "I take it that here in England, that rule, at least by the laws of England, is false; and therefore, if a person, being under necessity for want of victuals or clothes, shall upon that account clandestinely and *animo furandi* steal another man's goods, it is felony, and a crime by the laws of England punishable with death." (Hale, Pleas of the Crown, i. 54.) If, therefore, Lord Hale is clear—as he is—that extreme necessity of hunger does not justify larceny, what would he have said to the doctrine that it justified murder?

It is satisfactory to find that another great authority, second, probably, only to Lord Hale, speaks with the same unhesitating clearness on this matter. Sir Michael Foster, in the 3rd chapter of his Discourse on Homicide, deals with the subject of "homicide founded in necessity"; and the whole chapter implies, and is insensible unless it does imply, that in the view of Sir Michael Foster "necessity and self-defence" (which he defines as "opposing force to force even to the death") are convertible terms. There is no hint, no trace, of the doctrine now contended for; the whole reasoning of the chapter is entirely inconsistent with it.

[The Court discusses additional authorities that are in agreement with the position already articulated.]

Is there, then, any authority for the proposition which has been presented to us? Decided cases there are none. The case of the seven English sailors referred to by the commentator on Grotius and by Puffendorf has been discovered by a gentleman of the Bar, who communicated with my Brother Huddleston, to convey the authority (if it conveys so much) of a single judge of the island of St. Kitts, when that island was possessed partly by France and partly by this country, somewhere about the year 1641. It is mentioned in a medical treatise published at Amsterdam, and is altogether, as authority in an English court, as unsatisfactory as possible. The American case cited by my Brother Stephen in his Digest, from Wharton on Homicide, in which it was decided, correctly indeed, that sailors had no right to throw passengers overboard to save themselves, but on the somewhat strange ground that the proper mode of determining who was to be sacrificed was to vote upon the subject by ballot, can hardly, as my Brother Stephen says, be an authority satisfactory to a court in this country. . . .

The one real authority of former time is Lord Bacon, who, in his commentary on the maxim, "*necessitas inducit privilegium quoad jura privata*," lays down the law as follows:—"Necessity carrieth a privilege in itself. Necessity is of three sorts—necessity of conservation of life, necessity of obedience, and necessity of the act of God or of a stranger. First of conservation of life; if a man steal viands to satisfy his present hunger, this is no felony nor larceny. So if divers be in danger of drowning by the casting away of some boat or barge, and one of them get to some plank, or on the boat's side to keep himself above water, and another to save his life thrust him from it, whereby he is drowned, this is neither *se defendendo* nor by misadventure, but justifiable." On this it is to be observed that Lord Bacon's proposition that stealing to satisfy hunger is no larceny is hardly supported by Staundforde, whom he cites for it, and is expressly contradicted by Lord Hale in the passage already cited. And for the proposition as to the plank or boat, it is said to be derived from the canonists. At any rate he cites no authority for it, and it must stand upon his own. Lord Bacon was great even as a lawyer; but it is permissible to much smaller men, relying upon principle and on the authority of others, the equals and even the superiors of Lord Bacon as lawyers, to question the soundness of his dictum. There are many conceivable states of things in which it might possibly be true, but if Lord Bacon meant to lay down the broad proposition that a man may save his life by killing, if necessary, an innocent and unoffending neighbour, it certainly is not law at the present day.

There remains the authority of my Brother Stephen, who, both in his Digest and in his History of the Criminal Law, uses language perhaps wide enough to cover this case. The language is somewhat vague in both places, but it does not in either place cover this case of necessity, and we have the best authority for saying that it was not meant to cover it. If it had been necessary, we must with true deference have differed from him, but it is satisfactory to know that we have, probably at least, arrived at no conclusion in which if he had been a member of the Court he would have been unable to agree. Neither are we in conflict with any opinion expressed upon the subject by the learned persons who formed the commission for preparing the Criminal Code. They say on this subject:—

"We are certainly not prepared to suggest that necessity should in every case be a justification. We are equally unprepared to suggest that necessity should in no case be a defence; we judge it better to leave such questions to be dealt with when, if ever, they arise in practice by applying the principles of law to the circumstances of the particular case."

It would have been satisfactory to us if these eminent persons could have told us whether the received definitions of legal necessity were in their judgment correct and exhaustive, and if not, in what way they should be amended, but as it is we have, as they say, "to apply the principles of law to the circumstances of this particular case."

Now, except for the purpose of testing how far the conservation of a man's own life is in all cases and under all circumstances, an absolute, unqualified, and paramount duty, we exclude from our consideration all the incidents of war. We are dealing with a case of private homicide, not one imposed upon men in the service of their Sovereign and in the defence of their country. Now it is admitted that the deliberate killing of this unoffending and unresisting boy was clearly murder, unless the killing can be justified by some well-recognised excuse admitted by the law. It is further admitted that there was in this case no such excuse, unless the killing was justified by what has been called "necessity." But the temptation to the act which existed here was not what the law has ever called necessity. Nor is this to be regretted. Though law and morality are not the same, and many things may be immoral which are not necessarily illegal, yet the absolute divorce of law from morality would be of fatal consequence; and such divorce would follow if the temptation to murder in this case were to be held by law an absolute defence of it. It is not so. To preserve one's life is generally speaking a duty, but it may be the plainest and the highest duty to sacrifice it. War is full of instances in which it is a man's duty not to live, but to die. The duty, in case of shipwreck, of a captain to his crew, of the crew to the passengers, of soldiers to women and children, as in the noble case of the *Birkenhead*; these duties impose on men the moral necessity, not of the preservation, but of the sacrifice of their lives for others, from which in no country, least of all, it is to be hoped, in England, will men ever shrink, as indeed, they have not shrunk. It is not correct, therefore, to say that there is any absolute or unqualified necessity to preserve one's life. "*Necesse est at eam, non at vivam*," is a saying of a Roman officer quoted by Lord Bacon himself with high eulogy in the very chapter on necessity to which so much reference has been made. It would be a very easy and cheap display of commonplace learning to quote from Greek and Latin authors, from Horace, from Juvenal, from Cicero, from Euripides, passage after passage, in which the duty of dying for others has been laid down in glowing and emphatic language as resulting from the principles of heathen ethics; it is enough in a Christian country to remind ourselves of the Great Example whom we profess to follow. It is not needful to point out the awful danger of admitting the principle which has been contended for. Who is to be the judge of this sort of necessity? By what measure is the comparative value of lives to be measured? Is it to be strength, or intellect, or what? It is plain that the principle leaves to him who is to profit by it to determine the necessity which will justify him in deliberately taking another's life to save his own. In this case the weakest, the youngest, the most unresisting, was chosen. Was it more necessary to kill him than one of the grown men? The answer must be "No"—

"So spake the Fiend, and with necessity,
The tyrant's plea, excused his devilish deeds."

It is not suggested that in this particular case the deeds were "devilish," but it is quite plain that such a principle once admitted might be made the legal cloak for unbridled passion and atrocious crime. There is no safe path for judges to tread but to ascertain the law to the best of their ability and to declare it according to their judgment; and if in any case the law appears to be too severe on individuals, to leave it to the Sovereign to exercise that prerogative of mercy which the Constitution has intrusted to the hands fittest to dispense it.

It must not be supposed that in refusing to admit temptation to be an excuse for crime it is forgotten how terrible the temptation was; how awful the suffering; how hard in such trials to keep the judgment straight and the conduct pure. We are often compelled to set up standards we cannot reach ourselves, and to lay down rules which we could not ourselves satisfy. But a man has no right to declare temptation to be an excuse, though he might himself have yielded to it, nor allow compassion for the criminal to change or weaken in any manner the legal definition of the crime. It is therefore our duty to declare that the prisoners' act in this case was wilful murder, that the facts as stated in the verdict are no legal justification of the homicide; and to say that in our unanimous opinion the prisoners are upon this special verdict guilty of murder.

THE COURT then proceeded to pass sentence of death upon the prisoners.

Notes and Questions

1. A Strange and Unusual Case. The *Queen v. Dudley and Stephens* is a strange and unusual case on many fronts. The facts are absolutely gripping and heartbreaking. The result seems, I think, both somehow right but also harsh to many people (it has seemed that way to the majority of my students over the years.)

One additional strange and unusual fact about the case has to do with the name of the unfortunate boy, Richard Parker. In 1838, almost 50 years before the above case, Edgar Allen Poe wrote his only full-length novel, *The Narrative of Arthur Gordon Pym of Nantucket*. In that novel, a whaling ship sinks, and one of the members of the crew is killed and eaten by the other survivors as they await rescue. The name of the unfortunate crew member who was killed and eaten just happens to be Richard Parker. Further, a different Richard Parker also drowned when the *Francis Spaight* sank in 1846. (The survivors of that wreck practiced cannibalism as well, but that Richard Parker drowned in the sinking and therefore died before those acts occurred.) Purportedly, the tiger in Yann Martel's novel *The Life of Pi* was named Richard Parker due to these coincidences.

2. How do we know something is a crime? Throughout the above opinion, the Court and the learned commentators that it cites assume that murder and theft are crimes. We could probably add many other things to that list such as kidnapping, rape, perjury, treason, etc. But, how do they (and consequently how can we) know that?

The answer that would have been given for much of the Western legal tradition is that we should look to the law of nature and nature's God to determine whether something is a crime. For example, the Ten Commandments provide that murder and theft are indeed wrong, and the punishments meted out for those things by the Old Testament law tend to clearly indicate that these things are most certainly crimes. It is from this worldview that the Court and the commentators operate and therefore so easily assume these things to be crimes.

By contrast, law and economics does not have a higher source of law, such as the law of nature and nature's God, to draw upon in order to answer questions such as "What should and should not be a crime?" Judge Posner answers this question, rather, by reference to a number of issues, including primarily that something should be a crime when tort damages are insufficient to efficiently deter the conduct in question.[68]

Nevertheless, that answer begs the question. Why is stealing, for example, wrong in the first place? In the biblical worldview, the answer is obvious. It violates God's righteous standards. From a law and economics perspective, it is less obvious. The answer, however, is that stealing is wrong because it bypasses the market for goods, and rape is wrong because it bypasses the market for sex. "*Rape* bypasses the market in sexual relations (marital and otherwise) in the same way that theft bypasses markets in ordinary good and services."[69] Presumably murder is wrong because a person is not likely to sell you his life at any price.

Thus, without reference to any type of external or transcendental morality, law and economics attempts to classify certain acts as "wrong." Then, the acts become a crime as opposed to a tort also without reference to any transcendental standard, but rather merely because greater damages or penalties such as fines or imprisonment or even death are required to efficiently deter the activity.

What do you think? Are rape and theft wrong merely because they bypass their respective markets? Or, is there something deeper?

3. How do we set a proper punishment? How do we determine what the proper punishment should be for a particular crime? Under the biblical worldview, we look to the law of nature and nature's God, and specifically *The Bible*, to attempt to discern what the punishment should be. For example, the punishment for capital murder in *The Bible* is death, and apparently death alone.[70] The punishment for theft (and most other crimes) is restitution and corporal punishment.[71]

Law and economics, on the other hand, sets punishment for crimes much the same way it determines whether a particular act amounts to negligence or not—by reference to a formula that compares the likely benefit to the criminal of committing the crime with the proposed punishment multiplied by the likelihood that the criminal will be apprehended, tried, convicted, and actually punished for the crime.[72] Criminals are considered to be rational maximizers of their happiness, like all people, and therefore it is surmised that they roughly engage in something like a cost-benefit analysis before committing a crime. What do you think, are criminals that rational?

---

[68] Posner, *Economic Analysis of Law, supra*, 253-258 (9th ed. 2014).

[69] *Id.* at 254.

[70] *See, e.g.,* Genesis 1:26-27, 9:6; Numbers 35:30-34; Deuteronomy 17:6-7; Jeffrey C. Tuomala, *Christ's Atonement as the Model for Civil Justice*, 38 Am. J. Juris. 221 (1993); and Jeffrey C. Tuomala, *The Value of Punishment: A Response to Judge Richard L. Nygaard*, 5 Regent U. L. Rev. 13 (1995). Dean Tuomala's articles are excellent on these topics, and I would highly recommend them to you.

[71] *See, e.g.,* Exodus 22:1-4; Leviticus 6:1-5; Deuteronomy 25:1-3; and Proverbs 6:30-31.

[72] Posner, *Economic Analysis of Law* 256-267 (9th ed. 2014).

What do you think about these two methods of setting punishment for crimes? What does this imply about the goal or purpose of criminal law from a law and economics perspective? What about a Christian perspective?

4. The Goal and Purpose of Criminal Law. Typically, there are three possible goals put forward for criminal law: rehabilitation, deterrence, and retribution. Law and economics is very much focused on deterrence. The goal is to deter crime to an efficient level as it would probably be inefficient to attempt to deter all crimes.

The biblical goal or purpose for criminal law is retribution or punishment. The civil magistrate is God's servant on earth to exact vengeance. However, this does not mean that the biblical system does not provide for both rehabilitation and deterrence. It certainly does. But, importantly, it does not set these as the goal. Instead, they are achieved as byproducts of obediently punishing evildoers. For more on this, I would highly recommend to you Dean Tuomala's excellent articles: *Christ's Atonement as the Model for Civil Justice*, 38 Am. J. Juris. 221 (1993); and *The Value of Punishment: A Response to Judge Richard L. Nygaard*, 5 Regent U. L. Rev. 13 (1995).

5. What would you do? When I teach this case in class, I always ask the students what they would do. So, I now ask you. What would you do as the judge? Would you find necessity here? If not, would you find murder and thereby send these men to the gallows? (In those days, people did not spend years on death row awaiting execution.)

Judge Posner's answer to this question is very interesting.[73] He acknowledges that the victim would not sell his life at any price. However, he seems willing to allow a defense of necessity based upon an agreement. "If it could be shown that in advance of the voyage the members of the crew had agreed to the sacrifice of the weakest if that became necessary to save the others, there would be an economic argument for allowing a defense of necessity."[74] I assume that, further, Judge Posner might be willing to imply this agreement based upon the fact that "most people would think that at some point a sacrifice of one person so that others will live increases societal welfare."[75]

What about as the executive, what would you do? Would you pardon them or carry out the execution? The Crown pardoned the men in real life, so they were not executed. Is that the right decision from a biblical perspective? Doesn't blood pollute the land and require execution?

What would you do if you were Brooks, the third man in the boat? Would you join in the killing? The eating? Or, would you do something else? What would *The Bible* suggest you should do?

---

[73] *Id.* at 280-281.

[74] *Id.* at 281.

[75] *Id.* Judge Eaterbrook, a colleague of Judge Posner's on the Seventh Circuit and a law and economics devotee, would certainly seem to be willing to accept a defense of necessity here. Frank H. Easterbrook, *The Case of the Speluncean Explorers: Revisited*, 112 Harvard Law Review 1834, 1913-1917 (1999).

CHAPTER 6

DEBT, BANKRUPTCY, AND CORPORATE LAW

This chapter takes its name from a chapter in Judge Posner's book that also deals with these three topics: debt, bankruptcy, and corporate law. There are several topics that this chapter could consider, and I hope that, Lord willing, later editions of the book will consider many additional topics. However, at present, this chapter focuses primarily on bankruptcy because it provides us with a wonderful opportunity to evaluate the contrast between a biblical approach to law and Judge Posner's approach.

Judge Posner's book discusses bankruptcy law, and, as you have probably come to expect, the prominent issue is efficiency. What would an efficient bankruptcy system look like? On whom does it impose costs? Are those costs justified, and, of course, many similar other questions. It is not that these questions are bad, per se, but they start *in media res*. This is not surprising given the absence of a higher law view in law and economics. For Judge Posner, the closest thing to a higher law is efficiency and the market. Therefore, one just begins by looking at what is currently being done, asking whether it is efficient, what would the market do, etc., and moving on from there.

However, a Christian worldview of law requires that one begin with the law of nature and nature's God and consider what is God's view of bankruptcy and debt forgiveness. It is then incumbent upon human law-makers to fashion positive law that matches God's eternal law. The following is designed to help you to do this within the topic of bankruptcy by considering whether bankruptcy is biblical, what are the purposes of bankruptcy, and the scope of dischargeability.

I. Is Bankruptcy Biblical?

Not surprisingly, Christians get into financial troubles, and, therefore, may find themselves considering bankruptcy, just as unbelievers do. Just because the Lord God has regenerated someone does not mean that he is now immune from sin or hardships. The biggest difference is (or certainly should be) that, while an unbeliever likely will not care, a believer will often want to know what God thinks about filing bankruptcy. The believer is (or, again, should be) concerned with whether bankruptcy is biblical.

Similarly, a Christian legal professional may end up working in the area of debtor-creditor relations law, politics, or some other area touching on bankruptcy law. Further, all Christians have a duty to vote, and all Christians should be concerned as to whether we have just laws that are in accordance with God's law. Therefore, all Christians, whether in financial trouble or not, should be concerned with the question, "Is bankruptcy biblical?"

As a Christian legal professional whose career has centered around business, tax, and commercial law, I have often had believers come to me in times of financial strain inquiring about bankruptcy. Usually, they want to know something of the procedure and process of bankruptcy, such as how long it will take or what the results and consequences will be. Further, they are almost always concerned about whether it is a sin to file bankruptcy. In the following, I share what I have told them over the years. I hope that it will be helpful to you in both advising those considering bankruptcy and in evaluating what a just bankruptcy system would be like (and therefore getting closer to understanding what our bankruptcy system should be like in order to honor the Lord.) Finally, I hope that it will present a helpful contrast between a biblical view of law and the law and economics approach.

The Wicked Borrows but does not Repay

Psalm 37:21 is a good place to start in considering whether a Christian should file bankruptcy. It states "[t]he wicked borroweth, and payeth not again: [b]ut the righteous sheweth mercy, and giveth." Incurring a debt is the making of a promise—i.e., the promise to repay, and God's Word demands that promises be kept. *See, e.g., Exodus* 20:16, *Leviticus* 19:11, *Psalm* 15:1-4 and 58:3, *Proverbs* 6:16-19, *Ecclesiastes* 5:4-7, *Matthew* 5:33-37, *Ephesians* 4:25, and *Colossians* 3:9. Accordingly, the Christian considering bankruptcy is immediately faced with a dilemma—*The Bible* clearly teaches that borrowing and failing to repay is a sin and bankruptcy allows one to do just that.

Before moving to consider *The Bible*'s system of debt relief and thereby attempting to resolve this dilemma, it is good to consider *The Bible*'s command to keep one's word by repaying and the implications it has in this setting. We should always begin the analysis of any situation in life by asking what God has commanded of us. We should not begin by asking what God has commanded of others and attempt to hold them to that.

We must stand before God in judgment alone, and it is no answer to say, "I would have obeyed fully if everyone else around me would just act right." This is blame shifting, and it was one of the first consequences of the original sin in the garden—Adam and Eve recognized they were naked, they hid from God, and, immediately upon being confronted with their sins, they starting trying to blame shift. In this regard, we will fair no better than our original parents did. God sees through blame shifting and is not impressed by it. An obedient and responsible Christian should not start by blaming others or circumstances. An obedient and responsible Christian should want to begin by repenting and believing God for forgiveness, mercy, and grace.

Accordingly, the place to begin to answer this question is by noting that borrowing and not repaying is sin for which repentance is required. While it may be possible to get into financial distress where bankruptcy becomes a real possibility without sinning (say, for instance, if a person who has otherwise been perfectly financially responsible incurs a debilitating and expensive medical condition which costs him his job and causes him to incur medical bills that he cannot pay in order to stay alive,) in my experience, many people in financial distress did not get there without sin. They generally have incurred too much debt and spent too recklessly. To put it another way, they have not been good stewards with what God has entrusted to them. (And, I have experienced this first hand. I have not filed bankruptcy or failed to repay a creditor, but I have, at times, been a very poor steward of the financial resources with which God has entrusted me—incurring too much debt and spending recklessly.) Thus, they should begin with genuine repentance.

To put it another way, our disobedience (or our situation, even if not arrived at through disobedience) does not give us a claim on the grace and mercy of others. Mercy and grace to which one has a claim is, by definition, something other than mercy and grace. Our disobedience does not give us a claim on the obedience of others. Rather, our disobedience should lead us to repent, believe, and obey. It should cause us to be willing to entrust ourselves into the hands of God and suffer any consequences in a way that would honor Him. It should not make us think that we can demand grace, mercy, and obedience from other people. The issue of their obedience is between them and God. This is true in the realm of finances just as it is in virtually all of life.[76]

This is true notwithstanding the fact that *The Bible* commands lenders to be gracious, treating others as they would want to be treated themselves in a similar situation. God often imposes duties on both sides of a transaction or situation, and those duties are not dependent upon the other side fulfilling their duties. God commands wives to respect their husbands and husbands to love their wives, but neither commandment is dependent upon the other being fulfilled before it becomes effective. No husband can say, and honor God, "I

---

[76] The only possible exceptions to this lie within situations like the family. Obviously, I, as a father, am in a position to demand the obedience of my children. I can command them to forgive a brother or sister who has wronged them, particularly when they are younger and, therefore, more subject to my commands. Even if I have wronged one of them, I can demand and exhort them to obedience, which would include forgiving me because God commands us to be forgiving. However, I should never attempt to demand their obedience before my own. Thus, I should first repent to God and to them fully admitting my sin and attempting to make whatever restitution is available to me (which, in many cases, will only be an honest and contrite apology.) Then, I should fulfill my God-given role as father and exhort them to their biblical duties. That said, in my experience, children are quick to forgive in these situations and need little exhortation.

All of that said, the situation of father (or mother) and child has little application to the debtor-creditor situation. Rarely will the one who incurred the debt be in a position of authority and discipleship *over* the creditor to whom the debt is owed. Therefore, it is quite safe to say that the place for the vast majority of debtors to begin is with their responsibility before God to repay what they owe quite apart from whatever duties God might place on creditors.

will love you as soon as you finally start respecting me." God says love your wife. Period. It is not a contingent duty. Similarly, debtors may not say to creditors, "You have a duty to be gracious to me and to treat me like I want to be treated—therefore, you must forgive my debt." Debtors should begin with their own duties to God and to others, and, in this area, it is clear that the foundational duty is to repay what you have borrowed.

Therefore, in considering the issue of whether a Christian should file bankruptcy and in considering whether a legal system should include a system of bankruptcy, the starting point is a recognition that debts should be repaid. For a Christian considering bankruptcy, this will often mean repentance and financial counseling to make sure that the pattern that lead to the consideration of bankruptcy is not repeated. For a legal system that desires to be in accord with God's law, this means first making sure that the legal system has a robust and effective system for the enforcement and collection of legally owed debts. Once that is in place, then an institution of some system for debt relief is appropriate.

The Biblical System of Debt Relief

While it is often surprising to those who have not read the Old Testament law, *The Bible* contains a robust system of debt collection and relief. For a consideration of *The Bible*'s system of debt relief, the best place to begin is *Deuteronomy* 15:1-18.

Deuteronomy 15:1-18
King James Version

---

15 At the end of *every* seven years thou shalt make a release. [2] And this *is* the manner of the release: Every creditor that lendeth *ought* unto his neighbour shall release *it*; he shall not exact *it* of his neighbour, or of his brother; because it is called the Lord's release. [3] Of a foreigner thou mayest exact *it* *again*: but *that* which is thine with thy brother thine hand shall release; [4] Save when there shall be no poor among you; for the Lord shall greatly bless thee in the land which the Lord thy God giveth thee *for* an inheritance to possess it: [5] Only if thou carefully hearken unto the voice of the Lord thy God, to observe to do all these commandments which I command thee this day. [6] For the Lord thy God blesseth thee, as he promised thee: and thou shalt lend unto many nations, but thou shalt not borrow; and thou shalt reign over many nations, but they shall not reign over thee. [7] If there be among you a poor man of one of thy brethren within any of thy gates in thy land which the Lord thy God giveth thee, thou shalt not harden thine heart, nor shut thine hand from thy poor brother: [8] But thou shalt open thine hand wide unto him, and shalt surely lend him sufficient for his need, *in that* which he wanteth. [9] Beware that there be not a thought in thy wicked heart, saying, The seventh year, the year of release, is at hand; and thine eye be evil against thy poor brother, and thou givest him nought; and he cry unto the Lord against thee, and it be sin unto thee. [10] Thou shalt surely give him, and thine heart shall not be grieved when thou givest unto him: because that for this thing the Lord thy God shall bless thee in all thy works, and in all that thou puttest thine hand unto. [11] For the poor shall never cease out of the land: therefore I command thee, saying, Thou shalt open thine hand wide unto thy brother, to thy poor, and to thy needy, in thy land.

[12] *And* if thy brother, an Hebrew man, or an Hebrew woman, be sold unto thee, and serve thee six years; then in the seventh year thou shalt let him go free from thee. [13] And when thou sendest him out free from thee, thou shalt not let him go away empty: [14] Thou shalt furnish him liberally out of thy flock, and out of thy floor, and out of thy winepress: *of that* wherewith the Lord thy God hath blessed thee thou shalt give unto him. [15] And thou shalt remember that thou wast a bondman in the land of Egypt, and the Lord thy God redeemed thee: therefore I command thee this thing to day. [16] And it shall be, if he say unto thee, I will not go away from thee; because he loveth thee and thine house, because he is well with thee; [17] Then thou shalt take an aul, and thrust *it* through his ear unto the door, and he shall be thy servant for ever. And also unto thy maidservant thou shalt do likewise. [18] It shall not seem hard unto thee, when thou sendest him away free from thee; for he hath been worth a double hired servant *to thee*, in serving thee six years: and the Lord thy God shall bless thee in all that thou doest.

There is far too much in this passage for a thorough exegesis here. However, some issues regarding debt relief come immediately into view from this passage. First, debt relief in the Old Testament law is tied to the idea of the Sabbath Year. The Sabbath Year occurred every seventh year. Just as the seventh day was a day of rest to be kept holy, the Sabbath Year was a year of rest, also to be kept holy. As a part of the Sabbath Year, there is a forgiveness of debt and a manumission (or freeing) of bondservants or slaves.

Second, the debt relief in the Old Testament law was a universal grant of relief. It did not exclude any debt and it was not conditioned upon how the debt was incurred. The only limitation is with regard to membership within God's covenant people—those within the nation of Israel. Those outside the covenant were not entitled to debt relief and manumission. For those within the covenant, the debt relief and manumission described here appears to be absolute. Presumably, this and other benefits of being a part of God's people would have enticed others to want to join God's covenant people and to take note of the wonderful laws that God has given His people.[77]

This is remarkable for its demonstration of mercy and grace to all of the citizens of Israel, regardless of their wealth and social standing, and regardless of how the particular debt or debts in question were incurred. As

---

[77] *See, e.g.,* Deuteronomy 4:6-8.

R. J. Rushdoony points out, there were essentially two ways that one could fall into debt or, even more severely, bondservice: incurring a debt and being unable to pay it or being required to make restitution for theft (or possibly some other crime). "A man could be sentenced to bondservice to make restitution for an unpaid debt, or for theft."[78]

Accordingly, this law provided debt relief not only for the typical situation where a debt had been incurred in the general course of life and the debtor is unable to repay but also where the debt had been incurred through malfeasance of the debtor. A simple example from a passage of the Old Testament law dealing with theft will suffice to illustrate the point. Exodus 22 provides that "[i]f a man shall steal an ox, or a sheep, and kill it, or sell it; he shall restore five oxen for an ox, and four sheep for a sheep. . . . [H]e should make full restitution; if he have nothing, then he shall be sold for his theft."[79] There is an amazing demonstration of God's grace in the fact that even though he incurred his debt, which he could not repay and which resulted in his being sold, by committing a crime, he should still experience debt relief and go free of his bondservice in the seventh year.[80]

It is not entirely clear whether the manumission of bondservants is in the Sabbath Year or after six years of service regardless of when the Sabbath Year falls. Commentators appear to struggle with this question. Dr. Rushdoony states simply that "[a] release was necessary on the Sabbath or seventh year."[81] The *ESV Study Bible* states that "[t]he sabbatical year provides a limit to such slavery (cf. Ex. 21:2–6; Lev. 25:39–46)."[82] The *New American Commentary: Deuteronomy* asserts that the debtor-bondservant would serve "until either he had paid off his obligations or served for a six-year period (v. 12). Thereupon he was to be released from his economic bondage so that once again he could be free and independent."[83] Comparing *Deuteronomy* 15 with *Exodus* 21 and *Leviticus* 25, a somewhat complicated and nuanced system appears to result, the explication of which is beyond the scope of this chapter. Suffice it to say, for our purposes here, that, regardless of how the debt was incurred, bondservice for a period of no more than six years was required.

In summary, *The Bible* clearly provides a just and gracious system of society-wide debt relief. Normal debts were relieved in the Sabbath Year, which occurred every six years. Therefore, no debt would exceed six years in duration. Further, as a remedy for the collection and enforcement of debts, a debtor unable to pay his debt could be sold into bondservice. Regardless of

---

[78] Rousas John Rushdoony, *Commentaries on the Pentateuch: Deuteronomy* 233 (2008).

[79] *Exodus* 22:1-4.

[80] It is not entirely clear whether the release here is in the Sabbath Year or after six years of service regardless of when the Sabbath Year falls. Commentators appear divided on the point.

[81] Rushdoony, *Commentaries* 234.

[82] *The ESV Study Bible* 354 (2008).

[83] Eugene H. Merrill, *The New American Commentary (Volume 4): Deuteronomy* 245–246 (1994) (footnote omitted).

whether the debt was incurred innocently or through malfeasance, the debtor-bondservant would serve no more than six years. He would then go free from both his debt and the related bondservice. As the system of debt relief demonstrates, God's law is manifestly both just and gracious.

Comparing the U.S. System of Debt Relief with the Biblical System

Since *The Bible* provides for a system of debt relief, then filing for bankruptcy is not, per se, a sin. Further, it would seem that a just legal system should include a system of debt relief since the biblical system does. Therefore, a Christian can file for bankruptcy without sin. The issue will then be a comparison of the United States bankruptcy system with the system of debt relief found in *The Bible*.

An exhaustive comparison of this type is beyond the scope of this chapter. However, it is useful to note a couple of differences by way of example. The examples should give some type of framework for a Christian who is considering bankruptcy to use, in conjunction with his local church, to evaluate if and how he should proceed through the bankruptcy process.

Obviously, the United States bankruptcy system bears some similarities to the biblical system. For example, both clearly contemplate debt relief, and both seem to be based in part on the idea that people should be given a second chance and a fresh start. However, that being said, there are some significant differences. A couple of these are discussed below.

First, the biblical system of debt relief is society wide, and it is centered primarily around the Sabbath year. The U.S. system, on the other hand, is primarily debtor initiated.[84] This does present some significant issues that should be considered in comparing the systems. For example, creditors in the U.S. system will find planning more difficult than creditors under the biblical system because U.S. debt relief is not automatically triggered upon set intervals, but rather is triggered by the debtor deciding to file a voluntary petition for bankruptcy. Creditors can perhaps predict with some certainty how many debtors will file bankruptcy, etc., out of a given set of loans, but this is a far cry from the certainty of an every seventh year system as contemplated by *The Bible*.

Second, there are many debts that are not dischargeable in the U.S. system. Debts related to fraud and other malfeasance are not dischargeable, nor are student loan debts, among others.[85] The biblical system on the other hand appears to discharge all debts, regardless of how they are incurred. A debt incurred for fraud appears to be dischargeable just as a debt incurred more innocently.

---

[84] Debtors can also be "forced" into bankruptcy by the filing of an involuntary petition. However, these are quite rare and the vast majority of bankruptcies begin by the filing of a voluntary petition by the debtor.

[85] *See* 11 U.S.C. § 523.

All Christians should be concerned as to how these and other differences might indicate changes that need to be made in the U.S. system to bring it in line with the biblical ideal. Further, Christians contemplating bankruptcy, with the help of their churches and church leaders, should consider how these differences might impact how and if a Christian should proceed through the bankruptcy system. Finally, Christian legal professionals working in the area of debtor-creditor relations law should be particularly aware of the similarities and differences between the U.S. and biblical system of debt relief so that they can advocate for change where needed and properly advise Christian and other clients seeking debt relief.

Notes and Questions

1. What would you do? Do you prefer our system of debt relief or *The Bible*'s? Do you find *The Bible*'s system of debt relief to be both just and gracious? If you were crafting a system of debt relief for modern society based upon *The Bible*, what would it look like? What type of system of debt relief would law and economics style reasoning propose? How is that different than the biblical system?

2. What would you tell him? If a friend of yours came to ask you whether he should file bankruptcy, what would you tell him? Would you just consider pragmatic issues such as efficiency or would you consider moral or biblical issues as well?

3. Reforming the Bankruptcy Code? If you were a member of Congress, would you suggest reforms to the Bankruptcy Code based upon the biblical system of debt relief? If so, what would they be? How would you answer these questions differently from a law and economics perspective?

II. The Purposes of Bankruptcy

Charles J. Tabb and Jillian K. McClelland, *Living with the Means Test*
31 S. Ill. U. L.J. 463 (2007)

A cornerstone principle of consumer bankruptcy law in the United States historically has been to provide "the honest but unfortunate debtor . . . a new opportunity in life and a clear field for future effort, unhampered by the pressure and discouragement of preexisting debt." [*Local Loan Co. v. Hunt*, 292 U.S. 234, 244 (1934).] Until 2005, this "fresh start" policy was implemented through the medium of a generous, immediate, and largely freely available chapter 7 discharge.

However, in 2005, the worm turned. In April 2005, Congress enacted and President Bush signed into law the Bankruptcy Abuse Prevention and Consumer Protection Act of 2005 ("BAPCPA"), effective for cases filed on or after October 17, 2005. In name and in substance, the 2005 Amendments to the Bankruptcy Code reveal an intent to restrict filings that are not made as a last resort. Illustrative of the rhetoric is a press release for the House Committee on the Judiciary, in which Rep. Rick Boucher contended that the then-existing Chapter 7 liquidation provisions allowed debtors to treat bankruptcy as just another "financial planning tool and file for bankruptcy for simple convenience."

The Bankruptcy Code currently in effect reflects an underlying concern that too many debtors who could afford to repay some of their debts were taking advantage of a forgiving bankruptcy regime to obtain a fresh start or "head start," to borrow the pejorative phrase of the day to the detriment of the economy, or at least of their creditors. The stated goal of the 2005 Amendments to the Bankruptcy Code was to restore integrity to the system by preventing "abuse." The main restorative vehicle was the "means test," which in § 707(b)(2) creates a presumption of "abuse" that dictates dismissal or conversion of a chapter 7 case for these "can-pay" consumer debtors. . . .

BAPCPA "replaces the presumption in favor of granting the relief sought by the debtor with a presumption that abuse exists" unless the debtor is able to prove, through extensive documentation, that he should be allowed a fresh start. The statutory "presumption of abuse", moreover, forces even honest but unfortunate debtors to rebut a moral charge against them.

Notes and Questions

1. The Purpose of the Biblical System of Debt Relief. The purpose of the American bankruptcy system historically, and at least in part, lined up with the purpose of the biblical system of debt relief as manifested in the Sabbath Year, i.e., a new beginning. Of this, Dr. R. J. Rushdoony writes:

> An important aspect of the year of release is that it means a year of renewed opportunity. God does not allow men, if they obey His law, to destroy their future indefinitely. In Joseph Parker's words,
>
>> We must have the element of hopefulness in life: without hope we die. Tomorrow will be a day of ransom and liberty— if not tomorrow by the clock, yet tomorrow in feeling: already the dawn is upon our hearts, already we hear noises of a distant approach: presently a great gladness will descend upon

the soul. The child will be better in a day or
two; when the weather warms (the doctor
assures us), the life will be stronger. When
arrangements   now   in   progress   are
consummated—and they will be consummated
presently—the whole house will be lighted up
with real joy and thankfulness. So the spirit
speaks to itself; so the heart sings songs in the
night-time; so we live by hope and faith. ...

We find in this year of release what we
all need—namely, the principle of new chances,
new   opportunities,   fresh   beginnings.
Tomorrow—said the debtor or the slave—is the
day of release, and the next day I shall begin
again: I shall have another chance in life; the
burden will be taken away, the darkness will
be dispersed, and life shall be young again.
Every man ought to have more chances than
one, even in our own life. God has filled the
sphere of life with opportunities. The expired
week is dead and gone, and Christ's own
resurrection day comes with the Gospel of
hope, and the Gospel of a new beginning, the
Gospel of a larger opportunity; and the year
dies with proclamations from heaven, and Life
says, when it is not utterly lost,—I will begin
again: I will no longer blot the book of life: I will
write with a steady and careful hand.

Parker rightly stressed that the meaning of God's law here is
to give His covenant people fresh opportunities.[86]

This quote both adequately and eloquently captures the hope, beauty, and
invigorating grace of a new beginning and a fresh start.

This gracious legal provision also points us to and derives from an idea
that is even more fundamental to all of creation—the gospel of the Lord Jesus
Christ, which is portrayed as a release from slavery, a release from
overwhelming debt, and freedom and rest in Christ. The biblical Sabbath Year
and its concomitant release from debt and slavery pointed to that much greater
release from debt and slavery to be found in Christ.[87]

---

[86] Rousas John Rushdoony, *Commentaries on the Pentateuch: Deuteronomy* 225 (2008)
(*quoting* Joseph Parker, *The People's Bible, Numbers 27-Deuteronomy (Volume 4)* 240–41 (n.d.)).
[87] *See, e.g., Luke* 4:18-19.

The Bible clearly teaches that all people are slaves to sin until and if they are set free from that slavery to be slaves to righteousness and to Christ.[88] Just as the biblical debt relief system brought freedom from bondservice, the gospel brings freedom from bondservice or slavery to sin. "6 We know that our old self was crucified with him in order that the body of sin might be brought to nothing, *so that we would no longer be enslaved to sin.* 7 For one who has died has been set free from sin."[89] "17 But thanks be to God, that you *who were once slaves of sin* have become obedient from the heart to the standard of teaching to which you were committed [i.e., the gospel], 18 and, *having been set free from sin*, have become slaves of righteousness."[90] Therefore, every time a slave was set free (a manumission) under the Old Testament legal system, it taught something of the greater manumission from sin that would come through the death, burial, and resurrection of the Lord Jesus Christ.

Similarly, *The Bible* teaches that all people owe an overwhelming sin debt to God that could only be paid through the substitutionary atonement of Christ's death on the cross.[91] The Sabbath Year brought freedom from debts (even debts that resulted from grievous sin such as stealing), and the gospel brings freedom from the most grievous debt of all—the sin debt. "3 And you, who were dead in your trespasses and the uncircumcision of your flesh, God made alive together with him, having forgiven us all our trespasses, 14 by canceling the record of debt that stood against us with its legal demands. This he set aside, nailing it to the cross."[92] The *ESV Study Bible* note on Colossians 2:14 is very helpful in amplifying Paul's point:

> In the Greco-Roman world, the "record of debt" (Gk. *cheirographon*) was a written note of indebtedness. Paul uses this as a word picture to characterize each person's indebtedness to God because of sin. God himself has mercifully resolved this problem for all who put their faith in Jesus by taking this note and **nailing it to the cross**, where Jesus paid the debt. The image comes from the notice fastened to a cross by the Roman authorities, declaring the crime for which the criminal was being executed (see John 19:19–22).[93]

Accordingly, every time a person's debts were forgiven under the Old Testament system of debt relief, it was a picture of the relief to be had in Christ from the awful sin debt owed to God.

Lastly, the Sabbath Year, and its related debt relief and manumission, was meant to grant freedom and rest to God's people. Both the Sabbath Day and the Sabbath Year taught this. In the New Testament, we are told that the

---

88 *See, e.g., Romans 6.*
89 *Romans 6:6-7 (ESV) (emphasis added).*
90 *Id.* at 6:17-18 (emphasis added).
91 *See, e.g., Matthew 6:12, 18:21-35; Colossians 2:13-14.*
92 *Colossians 2:13-14 (ESV).*
93 *The ESV Study Bible 2297 (2008).*

Sabbath (presumably both the Sabbath Day and the Sabbath Year) find their ultimate fulfillment in the Lord Jesus Christ. Just as the freedom from debt and slavery should bring about a wonderful rest, so does the freedom from sin debt and slavery through the gospel bring about a wonderful rest. Again, the Old Testament law of Sabbath, or rest, taught about and pictured the coming rest in Christ.

In summary, the purpose of the biblical system of debt relief—giving the debtor freedom from debt and slavery and thereby a new beginning—on a deeper level is actually to teach people about and point to salvation through the Lord Jesus Christ. Accordingly, the principle underlying the biblical system of debt relief is in a very real way the gospel.[94]

2. An Additional Purpose? The American bankruptcy system also carries an additional purpose; one that is not as frequently stated as the "fresh start" purpose. The additional purpose is the orderly distribution of the debtor's non-exempt assets to his creditors. This is meant to prevent the so-called "race to the courthouse" where all of the debtor's creditors race to the courthouse to file suit and obtain liens. Obviously, the lien priority system is based in large measure upon a winner-take-all, first-in-time-first-in-right type philosophy that results in those who get their liens first getting completely paid and those who are late comers in the race to the courthouse getting nothing. Thus, the bankruptcy system is thought to be more equitable (or efficient?) in that it freezes the debtor's estate and equitably divides the assets among the various creditors. Accordingly, in the American system of debt relief, there is, in addition to the "fresh start" purpose, a repayment purpose. It is this repayment purpose that was at the heart of the BAPCPA's desire to prevent abuse.

3. Comparison of the Purpose of the Biblical System of Debt Relief with the American Bankruptcy System. As noted above, both the biblical system of debt relief and the American bankruptcy system share as an important purpose the granting of a second chance, a fresh start, to the debtor. However, the American system adds to this a repayment purpose that is not directly found in the biblical system.[95]

As the article excerpt at the beginning of this section points out, and as the Supreme Court has recently noted, the BAPCPA shifted the balance in the American bankruptcy system more toward repayment as opposed to a fresh start.

---

[94] Which helps to explain why the biblical system of debt relief was only available to God's covenant people, the Israelites, and was not available to those outside of God's people. Those outside of Christ do not have freedom from slavery to sin and their sin debt has not been paid. Therefore, they do not enjoy freedom and rest in Christ.

[95] *The Bible* strongly encourages the repayment of debts. Therefore, this should not be seen as hostility toward the repayment of debts in general. Rather, the Sabbath Year debt relief system does not attempt to combine the goal of the repayment of just debts with the purpose of a fresh start as the American system does.

"Congress enacted the . . . BAPCPA . . . to correct perceived abuses of the bankruptcy system." *Milavetz, Gallop & Milavetz, P.A. v. United States,* 559 U.S. 229, ——, 130 S.Ct. 1324, 1329, 176 L.Ed.2d 79 (2010). In particular, Congress adopted the means test—"[t]he heart of [BAPCPA's] consumer bankruptcy reforms," H.R.Rep. No. 109–31, pt. 1, p. 2 (2005), and the home of the statutory language at issue here—to help ensure that debtors who *can* pay creditors *do* pay them. *See, e.g., ibid.* (under BAPCPA, "debtors [will] repay creditors the maximum they can afford").[96]

Since the goal of repayment is not even really present in the biblical debt relief systems, a shift toward that goal in the American system requires thoughtful Christian reflection and evaluation. Is such a shift a sign of a movement away from biblical principles? How would this differ if one took a law and economics approach? Is this justified from an efficiency perspective?

This question necessarily requires some determination regarding abuse, the concern about which was at the heart of the BAPCPA reforms. The fact that the American bankruptcy system is debtor-initiated, as opposed to a set society-wide time of debt relief, arguably does open up the potential for abuse in a way not present in the biblical system.

In the biblical system, everyone would be aware of the coming of the Sabbath Year. "To protect both lender and borrower, the loan, one assumes, was of such an amount as to reasonably be repaid in whatever time remained until the year of cancellation [the Sabbath Year]. That is, the size of the loan was commensurate with the time to repay it."[97] In fact, given the nature of the system, God seems to have been more concerned that lenders would be unwilling to lend as the Sabbath Year drew nigh as opposed to debtors being able to abuse the system.[98]

By contrast, in the American bankruptcy system, a creditor is never quite sure when any particular debtor might file bankruptcy. Leaving the timing of debt relief in the hands of debtors does open up the possibility of opportunistic behavior or abuse of the system. Therefore, at least arguably, the dual (and often competing goal) of repayment is warranted in the American system. Further, and again arguably, a shift more toward repayment was perhaps warranted in 2005.

A thorough consideration of this difference (debtor-initiated debt relief v. society-wide at a particular time debt relief) and all of its implications is beyond the scope of this chapter (and likely the ability of this author.) Still, it seems that at least some consideration of this important distinction between the two systems is critical in order to think through this issue of purpose.

---

[96] *Ransom v. FIA Card Services, N.A.,* 559 U.S. 61, 64 (2011).

[97] Eugene H. Merrill, *Deuteronomy, The New American Commentary (Volume 4)* 243 (1994).

[98] *Deuteronomy* 15:7-11.

However, this begs a deeper question: maybe the discussion initially should be whether the American system should switch to the biblical model of a set time of society-wide debt relief as opposed to the current debtor-initiated system.

Regardless, these are very important issues and questions. The law is undoubtedly didactic, meaning that it teaches people. It can either teach people good lessons about things that are God-honoring, righteous, and true, or it can teach people lies about the nature of the world and the God who made it. In this instance, it seems that debt relief is, in *The Bible*, very much tied up in teaching people about the gospel. Therefore, all Christians should be concerned about our system of debt relief and what it is teaching.

What do you think? What does our system of debt relief in America teach? Is it subject to abuse? What should be done about that abuse if so? Should we shift the purpose and focus more toward repayment, as the BAPCPA did, or should we look at fundamentally changing the system?

If we did shift to the biblical system of a set time of society-wide debt relief, what might that look like? Can you imagine it? Could it possibly work, or is our current system better?

III. Nondischargeability and the Biblical Worldview

In re Marlow
2013 WL 3515726 (E.D. Tenn. July 11, 2013)

Robert Bentley Marlow has a law degree but no Tennessee law license. He also has nearly $250,000 in student loans that he asserts he cannot pay. After filing for bankruptcy, he sought a discharge of his student loans under 11 U.S.C. § 523(a)(8). The bankruptcy court found the debt was not dischargeable and granted summary judgment in favor of the United States Department of Education, Sallie Mae, Inc., the University of Tennessee, and Educational Credit Management Corporation (collectively, the "Appellees"). In making this ruling, the bankruptcy court found that Marlow could not satisfy the three prerequisites for relief under 11 U.S.C. § 523(a)(8). The bankruptcy court found Marlow had not maximized his income nor made a good faith effort to repay his student loans to the Appellees. Additionally, the bankruptcy found no additional circumstance indicating that Marlow's state of financial affairs is likely to persist for a significant portion of the repayment period.

Proceeding *pro se,* Marlow now appeals the decision of the bankruptcy court. Marlow argues that the bankruptcy court erred in its findings of fact and conclusions of law and that the Court should vacate the bankruptcy court's memorandum and judgment and remand for further proceedings. The Court has carefully reviewed the parties' briefs in light of the entire record and controlling law. For the reasons set forth below, the decision of the bankruptcy court will be affirmed and Marlow's appeal dismissed.

I.

Marlow was 31 years old at the time of the bankruptcy proceedings. By that time, he had several degrees. He earned a bachelor's degree in philosophy from the University of Tennessee in December 2001 and an associate's degree in paralegal studies from Roane State Community College in May 2004. He also earned a law degree from the Cumberland School of Law at Samford University in May 2009 and a master's degree in social and political philosophy from the University of Tennessee in May 2010. He financed these two advanced degrees with subsidized and unsubsidized federally funded student loans as well as private student loan obligations from the Appellees. The total of all loans to all Appellees at the time of the bankruptcy proceedings was $247,877.93.

After law school, Marlow failed the Tennessee bar exam in the summer of 2009. He took the exam again in February 2010, and he passed. The Tennessee Board of Law Examiners, however, did not admit him to the Tennessee bar. On April 2, 2010, Marlow was notified by letter that his application[for bar admission had been place[d] [*sic*] under investigation for character and fitness concerns based on his prior citation for public intoxication and his sixteen motor vehicle citations. Then, on April 21, 2010, Marlow was arrested by the Knoxville City Police for public intoxication. The Board of Law Examiners issued a show cause order on May 18, 2010, directing Marlow to show why his application should not be denied on character and fitness grounds. Marlow responded, but upon the advice of his father and uncle, two Tennessee attorneys, he did not disclose his most recent arrest. By the time of Marlow's response, the Board of Law Examiners had received an anonymous tip about the recent arrest, and so it scheduled the first show cause hearing on the matter. Marlow appeared at this first hearing, and he explained that criminal charges from the April 20, 2010 arrest were ultimately dismissed. He rejected two monitoring agreements proposed by the Tennessee Lawyers Assistance Program, and he did not appear at a second show cause hearing because he was in Japan on a trip with his sister.

Ultimately, on June 27, 2011, the Board of Law Examiners determined Marlow should not be licensed to practice law in Tennessee. Marlow appealed the decision, and on February 12, 2012, the Tennessee Supreme Court affirmed the decision. Marlow has not sought admission to practice law in any other state, and he has no plans to do so. He has continued to appeal the licensing decision by filing a Petition for Writ of Certiorari with the United States Supreme Court, which was denied on October 1, 2012. Additionally, Marlow has pursued separate civil litigation against the Board of Law Examiners.

After receiving deferments in 2009 and 2010, Marlow made minimal payments to Sallie Mae, Inc. He did not make payments on the other loans. He sought forbearance from the University of Tennessee in November 2010 and February 2011, and he requested forbearance concerning the loans now held by Educational Credit Management Corporation. Since receiving his law and master's degrees, Marlow has not had steady employment. His primary financial support has come from his father. Since April 2007, Marlow has held the position of co-founder and managing member of Dogwood Creek Investments, LLC, a real estate development company in Knoxville, Tennessee. Marlow estimates that he has earned $125.00 per month from Dogwood Creek Investments since September 2010. This is the final position listed on Marlow's resume, which mostly reflects Marlow's time as a student, and thus the six other entries from 2002 to 2009 are part-time or temporary positions and externships. Since law school, Marlow also has been self-employed: he has worked landscaping, construction, and various odd jobs, sold beverages outside Neyland Stadium during University of Tennessee football games in the fall of 2009 and 2010, and collected scrap metal and aluminum cans. In 2011, he earned income from payments on [a] promissory note he issued on January 5, 2011. In 2012, like in 2011, his limited income included gifts from family and friends.

Marlow voluntarily filed for Chapter 7 bankruptcy protection on August 29, 2011, primarily for relief from his student loan debt, as well as some credit card debt. At that time, he listed in his bankruptcy schedules a total unsecured debt of $260,453.36, of he which listed $223,542.00 owed to the Appellees for student loans. Marlow then sought to discharge his student loan debt pursuant to 11 U.S.C. § 523(a)(8). The bankruptcy court determined that this debt could not be discharged, and this appeal followed.

* * *

III.

As Marlow correctly notes, the bankruptcy court's findings of fact are subject to a clearly erroneous standard of review, Bankruptcy Rule 8013, and its conclusions of law are subject to a *de novo* standard of review. *Oyler v. Educ. Credit Mgmt. Corp. (In re Oyler)*, 397 F.3d 382, 384 (6th Cir.2005). The Sixth Circuit Court of Appeals has stated that "[w]hether student loans pose an undue hardship is a legal question" for *de novo* review. *Id.*

Student loan debt may be discharged only when repayment "will impose an undue hardship on the debtor and the debtor's dependents." 11 U.S.C. § 523(a)(8). The Sixth Circuit has adopted the *Brunner* test for undue hardship which requires a three-part showing:

(1) that the debtor cannot maintain, based on current income and expenses, a 'minimal' standard of living for herself and her dependents if forced to repay the loans;

(2) that additional circumstances exist indicating that this state of affairs is likely to persist for a significant portion of the repayment period of the student loans; and

(3) that the debtor has made good faith efforts to repay the loans.

Tirch v. Pa. Higher Educ. Assistance Auth. (In re Tirch), 409 F.3d 677, 680 (6th Cir.2005) (quoting *Brunner v. N.Y. State Higher Educ. Serv. Corp.*, 831 F.2d 395 (2d Cir.1987)); *Oyler*, 397 F.3d at 385. "If a plaintiff cannot satisfy even one of these criteria, then she is not entitled to a finding of undue hardship." *Miller v. Pa. Higher Educ. Assistance Agency (In re Miller)*, No. 3:05–cv–38, 2005 WL 2127931, at *3 (E.D.Tenn. Aug.31, 2005). Upon review of the record, the Court finds that the bankruptcy court correctly concluded that Marlow cannot meet his burden under all of the prongs of the *Brunner* test.

To satisfy the first prong, a debtor must show that he strives to minimize his expenses and maximize his income. After reviewing the undisputed facts taken from Marlow's own discovery responses, and citing Marlow's own admissions, the bankruptcy court found that Marlow had minimized his expenses but failed to maximize his income. The bankruptcy [court] emphasized that he admitted to performing only a "cursory look for jobs on several online jobs boards and found no jobs that match his credentials" since February 2012. This "cursory look" was the result of his choice to devote his time to *pro se* lawsuits against the Tennessee Supreme Court and its members, the Tennessee Board of Law Examiners and its members, the Tennessee Attorney General, the City of Knoxville, and the officer who arrested him. In addition, the bankruptcy court noted that Marlow had not sought to obtain a law license outside Tennessee nor had he sought employment outside of Knoxville, where he resides. Overall, the bankruptcy court found Marlow's pursuit of employment to be limited at best, and this Court agrees. Marlow's own discovery responses and admissions create a clear record showing a failure to maximize his income, and so he has failed to satisfy the first of the *Brunner* prongs.

The second prong of the *Brunner* test requires a debtor to show that additional circumstances exist indicating that the state of affairs that prevents him from repaying his student loans is likely to persist for a significant portion of the repayment period. The focus, therefore, is on "permanency or, what can be termed, an involuntary inability to improve one's financial circumstances." *Storey v. Nat'l Enter. Sys. (In re Storey)*, 312 B.R. 867, 871 (Bankr.N.D.Ohio 2004). To meet this prong, Marlow must show "a certainty of hopelessness, not merely a present inability to fulfill financial commitment." *Tirch*, 409 F.3d at 681; *Oyler*, 397 F.3d at 386. The Sixth Circuit has explained that the additional circumstances "may include illness, disability, a lack of useable job skills, or the existence of a large number of dependents." *Oyler*, 397 F.3d at 386. Above all, the additional circumstances "must be beyond the debtor's control, not borne of free choice." *Id.; see also Barrett v. Educ. Credit Mgmt. Corp. (In re Barrett)*, 487 F.3d 353, 358 (6th Cir.2007).

In this case, Marlow is not suffering from any illness or disability, and he has no dependents. At the time of the bankruptcy proceedings, he was 31 years old. He is clearly well-educated. He has useable job skills, including his training as a paralegal. Here, Marlow offers the denial of his application for a Tennessee law license as an additional circumstance indicating his financial situation is likely to persist. The bankruptcy court held that this was not the type of circumstance required under *Brunner,* and this Court agrees. The denial of his application was the result of actions taken by Marlow, actions "borne of free choice." Marlow has not provided evidence that his lack of a law license makes him unemployable in any of his fields of expertise. "The Court, therefore, cannot say that [his] past will inevitably and ultimately result in a complete restriction, as opposed to a potential narrowing, of job opportunities in [his] profession." *Nixon v. Key Educ. Res. (In re Nixon),* 453 B.R. 311, 332 (Bankr.S.D.Ohio 2011) (discussing a debtor whose degree was revoked for plagiarism). Moreover, the record is clear that Marlow has not sufficiently sought to maximize his income. The bankruptcy court examined this record in detail and concluded that Marlow has not presented evidence that he exhausted all reasonable efforts to obtain non-legal employment. Marlow's efforts actually were focused on his *pro se* litigation, not finding employment. Given the clearly supported facts, the existence of Marlow's financial circumstances do not evidence an undue hardship.

The third prong of the *Brunner* test requires a debtor to show that he has made good faith efforts to repay his student loans. In finding that Marlow had not attempted to repay his loans in good faith, the bankruptcy court considered factors drawn from *Hart v. Educ. Credit Mgmt. Corp. (In re Hart),* 438 B.R. 406, 413 (E.D.Mich.2010):

> (1) whether the failure to repay the student loan was due to circumstances beyond the debtor's reasonable control; (2) whether the debtor has used all available resources to repay the loan; (3) whether the debtor is using her best efforts to maximize her earnings potential; (4) how long after the loan was incurred did the debtor seek to discharge the debts; (5) what the overall percentage of the student loan debt is compared to debtor's overall debt; and (6) whether or not the debtor has gained tangible benefits of the student loan.

Here, the factors clearly support the bankruptcy court's determination. As discussed above, Marlow's failure to repay is not beyond his reasonable control. He has declined to apply for an income contingent repayment plan, so he has not used all available resources to repay the loans. Marlow has made almost no payments on his loans, turning to the bankruptcy court for relief just over a year after obtaining his fourth degree. Marlow's student loan debt comprises the majority (approximately 86%) of his overall debt, and he has received a tangible benefit from these student loans in the form of two advanced degrees.

Considering the record, especially the timing of his bankruptcy filing, his minimal payments, and his failure to seek income-based repayment plans, Marlow has failed to show he made a good faith effort to repay his loans. *See also Fields v. Sallie Mae Serv. Corp., et al. (In re Fields)*, 286 F. App'x 246, 251 ("Moreover, because Fields declined even to apply for [income contingent repayment] relief, she has failed to sustain the 'heavy burden' under *Tirch* of proving that she made a good faith effort to repay her loans."). The Court therefore agrees with the bankruptcy court that Marlow cannot meet the third prong of the *Brunner* test.

As discussed above, a debtor must meet all three *Brunner* prongs to be eligible for an undue hardship discharge of his student loans. This Court agrees with the bankruptcy court that there is no genuine dispute of material fact that would enable Marlow to meet his burden with respect to every *Brunner* prong, and thus summary judgment in favor of the Appellees was proper. Accordingly, the Court affirms the opinion of the bankruptcy court, and Appellant Robert Bentley Marlow's appeal will be dismissed.

Notes and Questions

1. What Do You Think? Do you agree with the Court, or would you have ruled differently? Does Mr. Marlow deserve a discharge of his student loans, or should he be forced to pay them? Why? If he does deserve a discharge, should it be partial or complete?

What would biblical principles require? How would you answer the above from a law and economics perspective? What are the relative costs and benefits to society?

2. A Growing Problem? Student loan debt has likely reached a crisis level in America. It is widely recognized by a number of sources, including the Federal Reserve Bank of New York and the Consumer Finance Protection Bureau, that student loan debt exceeds $900 billion and may well be at or over $1 trillion. That exceeds credit card debt, auto loan debt, and home equity line of credit debt. Only home mortgage debt exceeds student loan debt for American households.[99]

Further, it is estimated that in excess of 25% of student loans have past due balances. Accordingly, it seems likely that there will be many, many more borrowers with student loan debt hoping to discharge all or part of their balances in bankruptcy. Many of these borrowers were undoubtedly strongly encouraged to pursue post-secondary or even post-graduate education, and, indeed, it is government policy that they should be so encouraged. That being said, does it make sense to except student loans from discharge? What policy is behind § 523(a)(8)? Do you agree with it? To put it another way, why are student loans treated differently than credit cards, auto loans, or home loans?

3. What Should the Test for Undue Hardship Be? "There has been a wide range of judicial reaction to the undue hardship claims of debtors. [However, t]he most widely used test for evaluating the dischargeability of a

---

[99] A simple Google search will reveal a number of sources on this topic, including the estimated number of student loans that are in arrears.

student loan under section 523(a)(8)" is the *Brunner* test, which has been adopted by the Sixth Circuit and was applied by the Court in the preceding case.[100]

Commenting on § 523(a)(8) and the federal courts' handling thereof, *Collier on Bankruptcy[101]* states

> Despite the courts' best efforts to formulate objective criteria for evaluating undue hardship, the application of the articulated standards necessarily requires each court to apply its own intuitive sense of what is a "minimal" standard of living and what is "good faith." At bottom, *the Bankruptcy Code requires bankruptcy courts to decide how much personal sacrifice society expects from individuals who accepted the benefits of guaranteed student loans but who have not obtained the financial rewards they had hoped to receive as a result of their educational expenditures.[102]*

Under § 523(a)(8) and Sixth Circuit precedent, there is no question that the Court arrived at the right answer in the preceding case. It correctly applied the *Brunner* test as adopted by the Sixth Circuit. That said, do you agree with the law on this point? Should it be more forgiving or less? Or, is it about right? Is this an objective standard that can be applied justly across all cases, or is it too subjective? To paraphrase the words of *Collier on Bankruptcy*, how much personal sacrifice should be expected of individuals who have accepted the benefits of guaranteed student loans and found themselves unable to repay? How would your answers to these questions change if you use a law and economics approach as opposed to a biblical approach?

4. *Factors v. Elements.* Some tests articulated by courts contain factors and others contain elements. The distinction is important. A test based upon factors typically requires a weighing of the various factors, but not all factors must be found in order for the test to have been met and typically no one factor is determinative. By contrast, in a test based upon elements, all elements must be satisfied.

The case above contains an example of both types of tests. Which test is based upon elements? Which one is based upon factors? Can you tell how this makes a difference?[103] Which appears to more consistent with a biblical worldview? What about the law and economics worldview?

5. *Discharge in the Biblical Debt Relief System.* As noted earlier, in the biblical system of debt relief, discharge appears to be complete. In other words, determinations of dischargeability are not made in the biblical debt

---

[100] 4 *Collier on Bankruptcy* ¶ 523.14[2] (Alan N. Resnick & Henry J. Sommer eds., 16th ed. 2009).

[101] *Collier on Bankruptcy* is probably the leading treatise on bankruptcy law.

[102] *Id.* (emphasis added.)

[103] *See, e.g., In re Fields*, 286 Fedd.Appx. 246, 251 (6th Cir. 2007) (*citing In re Oyler*, 397 F.3d 382, 386-386 (6th Cir. 2005)).

relief systems because all debts appear to be subject to discharge. As noted previously in this chapter, the biblical system forgives all debts however incurred. This is very much like the gospel, which forgives all of the sin debt owed regardless of the type of sins that comprise that debt. *See, e.g., Mark* 3:28-29 ("[a]ll sins shall be forgiven unto the sons of men, and blasphemies wherewith soever they shall blaspheme"); 1 *John* 1:9 ("[i]f we confess our sins, he is faithful and just to forgive us *our* sins, and to cleanse us from all unrighteousness"); and 1 *Corinthians* 6:11 (after listing off a number of heinous sins, Paul tells the Corinthians "such were some of you: but ye are washed, but ye are sanctified, but ye are justified in the name of the Lord Jesus, and by the Spirit of our God").[104]

Accordingly, it could be argued that a just system of debt relief based upon the biblical model would also forgive all debts. Discharge would therefore be complete, and there would be no issues of nondischargeability. However, as noted previously, this raises the very challenging issue of the primary difference between the biblical system of debt relief and the American bankruptcy system, i.e., the fact that the American system is debtor-initiated as opposed to being society wide as in the biblical system. How should this difference impact the American bankruptcy system? Is a concern with nondischargeability legitimate given the fact that bankruptcy is debtor-initiated and therefore more subject to abuse by debtors? Or, regardless of this difference, should the American system still provide for a complete discharge?

Beyond this difference, another difference should be considered in making this determination. The biblical system also provides for more robust (to say the least) debt collection methods. Under the biblical system, one could be sold into bondservice if he could not pay for his debts. *See, e.g., Deuteronomy* 15:12-18, *Leviticus* 25:35-55, and 2 *Kings* 4:1-7. His service (or the price of his service) would help to repay what he owed.

Obviously, in the present case, Mr. Marlow (or his father) would be much more interested in paying his debts if he thought he would be sold into bondservice if he could not pay. Further, he would likely have been much more cautious with regard to both incurring the debt and engaging in activities that cost him the opportunity to become a licensed attorney and to practice law.

Since debt collection methods under the biblical system were more drastic, a broader discharge was perhaps justified. On the other hand, in our system, where debt collection methods are not so robust, more of a focus on debt repayment, in addition to a fresh start for the debtor, coupled with the nondischargeability of certain debts is perhaps necessary. What do you think? Does this difference in debt collection possibilities between the biblical and American systems necessitate differences with regard to both the purpose of bankruptcy and the issue of the scope of the discharge available? Which

---

[104] The unforgivable sin described in *Mark* 3:29, in the opinion of the author, is the one exception, which can only be committed by one so hardened that salvation through Christ has already been undeniably rejected.

system is more just? Which is more efficient or which maximizes societal wealth? Which system do you prefer?

CHAPTER 7

THE REGULATION OF FINANCIAL MARKETS

It is difficult to overstate the importance of the United States' capital market to the national and international economies. This fact was dramatically illustrated in the 2008 financial crisis where a panic in a rather small corner of the United States' securities markets set off a chain reaction that affected not only large Wall Street firms, like Bear Stearns, but also smaller firms and individuals on "Main Street" and indeed around the world. Firms and individuals that were in no way connected with mortgage-backed securities, credit default swaps, and the other instruments that set off the crisis were profoundly impacted nonetheless, and, in many ways, at the writing of these words neither the United States' nor the world economy has fully recovered from the so-called "Great Recession." Literally, the United States' securities markets have the power to affect the lives of nearly every person on the globe, for good or ill.

The law governing an area this important to the functioning of the world economy and to the lives of virtually all people on the planet needs the application of the Christian worldview. Unfortunately, to date, very little Christian worldview thinking and analysis has been done in the realm of securities regulation. Certainly, this chapter does not pretend to such a lofty goal of providing all of the necessary Christian worldview analysis in this area, nor am I capable of attaining such a goal. Rather, the purpose of this article is to attempt to lay out some fundamental principles that could perhaps provide a framework for a biblical worldview of securities regulation and therefore provide some point of comparison with the law and economics approach. Further, it might provide a framework for how Christians might approach issues of law and policy in this important area in a manner consistent with the law of nature and nature's God.

I. Why Treat Financial Markets Differently?

Traditionally, in the Western legal tradition, markets and commercial activity are left largely unregulated in the sense that the present securities regulation regime regulates the securities markets. The present securities regulation regime has two primary pieces: mandatory disclosure and antifraud provisions.[105]   Fraud is within the role of the civil magistrate under a Christian worldview and has been recognized as being actionable or punishable at common law.   As far as that goes, the regulation of securities markets is not different from the regulation of commercial activity in general. However, there are special rules, such as the "fraud-on-the-market" rule, that are very much unlike anything seen at common law.

However, the real difference in how we regulate securities markets as opposed to commercial activity in general comes in the area of required disclosure.   Broadly speaking, disclosure is not required in any way by the seller in traditional markets, although the law has been moving away from this in recent times.   This idea is embodied in the phrase *caveat emptor*, or "buyer beware."   Further, if the buyer has special knowledge, he is not required to make a disclosure of that either.   Again, generally speaking, the Western legal tradition punishes fraud (and by that I mean activity that amounts to common law fraud) and otherwise leaves the parties to negotiate and evaluate deals for themselves.

This traditional approach of the Western legal tradition to the regulation of commercial activity and markets is illustrated in the Parable of the Hidden Treasure found in Matthew 13:44.[106]   In this short parable, Jesus said, "The kingdom of heaven is like treasure hidden in a field, which a man found and covered up.   Then in his joy he goes and sells all that he had and buys that field."[107]

Jesus told the Parable of the Hidden Treasure to his disciples after "he left the crowds and went into the house."[108]   He had been instructing the crowds with parables while sitting beside the Sea of Gaillee, but this parable he told to his disciples alone, along with the other parables and the explanation of the Parable of the Weeds found in Matthew 13:36-52.[109]   The Parable of the Pearl of Great Value, found in the next two verses, is similar to the Parable of the Hidden Treasure.[110]   It reads, "[a]gain, the kingdom of heaven is like a merchant in search of fine pearls, who, on finding one pearl of great value, went and sold all that he had and bought it."[111]

Both of these parables teach primarily the enormous value that should be assigned to salvation and entering the kingdom of heaven.   Espousing this traditional understanding of the parables, John Calvin wrote the following:

---

[105] At times these overlap to some degree.   For example, it is primarily from the anti-fraud provisions that the requirement to disclose or abstain from trading comes because that duty comes from Section 10(b) of the Securities Exchange Act of 1934 and Rule 10b-5 promulgated thereunder.   Thus, a rule of disclosure is derived from a federal securities regulation anti-fraud provision.

[106] Matthew 13:44.

[107] *Id.* (ESV).

[108] Matthew 13:36 (ESV).

[109] Matthew 13:1-35.

[110] Matthew 13:45-46.

[111] *Id.*

The first two of these parables are intended to instruct believers to prefer *the Kingdom of heaven* to the whole world, and therefore to deny themselves and all the desires of the flesh, that nothing may prevent them from obtaining so valuable a possession. We are greatly in need of such a warning; for we are so captivated by the allurements of the world, that eternal life fades from our view; and in consequence of our carnality, the spiritual graces of God are far from being held by us in the estimation which they deserve. Justly, therefore, does Christ speak in such lofty terms of the excellence of eternal life, that we ought not to feel uneasiness at relinquishing, on account of it, whatever we reckon in other respects to be valuable.

. . .

. . . The same instruction is conveyed by the other parable. *One pearl,* though it be small, is so highly valued, that a skillful *merchant* does not hesitate to *sell* houses and lands in order to purchase it. The excellence of the heavenly life is not perceived, indeed, by the sense of the flesh; and yet we do not esteem it according to its real worth, unless we are prepared to deny, on account of it, all that glitters in our eyes.[112]

However, beyond this primary meaning, both of these parables present the actions of the men (the treasure finder and the pearl merchant) in a positive light, assuming these actions are worthy of imitation. Notably and most relevant to the issue at hand, the treasure finder is not condemned, but rather seems to be praised, for purchasing the field without making disclosure. Certainly, he is in possession of material nonpublic information regarding the field that the owner-turned-seller of the field does not possess, i.e., that it contains treasure. Further, one could easily imagine what would have happened had disclosure been made—the treasure would have been removed from the field prior to its sale. Therefore, it is reasonable to conclude that Jesus recognized the current state of the law at that time, i.e., that disclosure was not required, and did not condemn it. Accordingly, it is also reasonable to conclude that the law of nature and nature's God does not therefore contain a general duty to disclose or abstain in commercial transactions.

Obviously, not all commentators would agree with this. For example, Craig Bloomberg writes:

---

[112] John Calvin, *Commentary on a Harmony of the Evangelists, Matthew, Mark, and Luke—Volume 2*, Matthew 13:44-52 (trans. William Pringle). For commentators sharing this traditional understanding of these parables, *see, e.g.,* Crossway Bibles, *The ESV Study Bible* 1849 (2008); Matthew Henry, *Matthew Henry's Commentary on the Whole Bible: Complete and Unabridged in One Volume* 1681–1682 (1994); and Craig Blomberg, *Matthew, vol. 22, The New American Commentary* 223–224 (1992).

One should not worry about the man's ethics in hiding the treasure. We need neither justify his behavior nor imitate it. This is simply part of the story line that helps to make sense of the plot. Jesus frequently tells parables in which unscrupulous characters nevertheless display some virtue from which Christians can learn (cf. esp. Luke 16:1–8; 18:1–8).[113]

Bloomberg argues that Jesus is merely using a plot device here and nothing more should be made of it. For support, he cites two other parables found in Luke 16:1-8 (The Parable of the Dishonest Manager) and Luke 18:1-8 (The Parable of the Persistent Widow). These parables certainly do involve what might be called negative examples—unrighteous characters whose actions teach something but whose morals should not be imitated. Or, as Bloomberg says, "unscrupulous characters [who] nevertheless display some virtue from which Christians can learn."[114]

However, a careful comparison of the parables indicates that Bloomberg's understanding of ethical or legal significance of the absence of disclosure in the Parable of the Hidden Treasure may be incorrect. To make this careful comparison, it is necessary to read the parables in their entirety. The Parable of the Unrighteous Steward provides:

> He also said to the disciples, "There was a rich man who had a manager, and charges were brought to him that this man was wasting his possessions. And he called him and said to him, 'What is this that I hear about you? Turn in the account of your management, for you can no longer be manager.' And the manager said to himself, 'What shall I do, since my master is taking the management away from me? I am not strong enough to dig, and I am ashamed to beg. I have decided what to do, so that when I am removed from management, people may receive me into their houses.' So, summoning his master's debtors one by one, he said to the first, 'How much do you owe my master?' He said, 'A hundred measures of oil.' He said to him, 'Take your bill, and sit down quickly and write fifty.' Then he said to another, 'And how much do you owe?' He said, 'A hundred measures of wheat.' He said to him, 'Take your bill, and write eighty.' The master commended *the dishonest* manager for his shrewdness. For the sons of this world are more shrewd in dealing with their own generation than the sons of light. And I tell you, make friends for yourselves by means of unrighteous wealth, so that when it fails they may receive you into the eternal dwellings.

---

[113] Blomberg, *Matthew* 223.
[114] *Id.*

>One who is faithful in a very little is also faithful in much, and one who is dishonest in a very little is also dishonest in much. If then you have not been faithful in the unrighteous wealth, who will entrust to you the true riches? And if you have not been faithful in that which is another's, who will give you that which is your own? No servant can serve two masters, for either he will hate the one and love the other, or he will be devoted to the one and despise the other. You cannot serve God and money. [115]

In this parable Jesus clearly indicates that the manager is in fact dishonest.[116] He has not been faithful with the wealth of another that was entrusted to him.[117] Jesus commends not his actions and his dishonesty to his hearers but rather his shrewdness in using the resources at his disposal to win for himself favor.[118] Jesus makes it abundantly clear that his actions should not be imitated, only his shrewdness.

Similarly, the Parable of the Persistent Widow does contain an unrighteous character, but, again, Jesus clearly indicates the character's unrighteousness.

>And he told them a parable to the effect that they ought always to pray and not lose heart. He said, "In a certain city there was a judge *who neither feared God nor respected man.* And there was a widow in that city who kept coming to him and saying, 'Give me justice against my adversary.' For a while he refused, but afterward he said to himself, *'Though I neither fear God nor respect man,* yet because this widow keeps bothering me, I will give her justice, so that she will not beat me down by her continual coming.'" And the Lord said, "Hear what *the unrighteous judge* says. And will not God give justice to his elect, who cry to him day and night? Will he delay long over them? I tell you, he will give justice to them speedily. Nevertheless, when the Son of Man comes, will he find faith on earth?"[119]

In this parable, as in the Parable of the Dishonest Manager, the character who is unrighteous is clearly presented as such. Jesus tells us that the judge

---

[115] Luke 16:1-13 (ESV) (emphasis added).

[116] Luke 16:8.

[117] Luke 16:10-12. In 1 Corinthians 4:1-2, the Apostle Paul recognizes that the law requires that managers, or stewards, are to be found faithful. Here, Paul also recognizes the current state of the law by using it as a positive example and without criticizing it, presumably indicating his approval thereof. Accordingly, it is reasonable to conclude that it is part of the law of nature and nature's God that stewards, and similarly agents, should be found faithful in their service to their masters.

[118] Luke 16:8-12.

[119] Luke 18:1-8 (ESV) (emphasis added).

"neither fear[s] God nor respect[s] man"[120] and calls him "the unrighteous judge."[121]

Further, the unrighteous judge does not fit Bloomberg's category of an "unscrupulous character[] [who] nevertheless display[s] some virtue from which Christians can learn." [122] In the Parable of the Persistent Widow, the judge's actions are not to be imitated by the Christian. The Christian is rather to imitate the widow by "always [] pray[ing] and not los[ing] heart."[123] In other words, the Christian is to imitate the virtue of the persistent widow by being persistent in prayer to God as she was persistent in her prayer to the unrighteous judge for justice.

The unrighteous judge, by contrast, is not to be emulated at all. Rather, he is compared to God, who "gives justice to his elect"[124] and does so "speedily."[125] The point of the comparison of the unrighteous judge to God can be summed up as "[i]f an unjust judge finally grants the widow's 'prayer,' how much more will God hear the prayers of his elect?"[126] God grants the prayers of his elect due to his righteousness and goodness while the unrighteous judge only acts out of annoyance at the widow's persistence.

This stands in stark relief to the Parable of the Hidden Treasure. The treasure finder is never condemned as being unrighteous as was the unrighteous judge and the dishonest manager. Further, his actions are presented in a positive light and as being worthy of imitation. Finally, Jesus seems to be taking a principle of law in existence at that time and using it to make a point without condemning the principle of law. All of this provides excellent support for the proposition that the duty to disclose material nonpublic information does not exist in the law of nature and nature's God and therefore did not exist at common law.

The difference between commercial transactions in most marketplaces (as discussed above) and the special regulation of securities markets is clearly presented in the case *SEC v. Texas Gulf Sulphur Co.*[127] While this case has a rather complicated factual situation that is exhaustively reported in a lengthy opinion, for the purposes of this article, it may be stated simply.

Texas Gulf Sulphur ("TGS"), a company engaged in mineral exploration and mining operations, discovered a very large ore deposit in eastern Canada in an area designated as the Kidd 55 segment.[128] The company took special care to keep the ore deposit discovery secret in order to "acquire the remainder of the Kidd 55 segment."[129] To state it a bit differently, TGS

---

[120] Luke 18:2 and 4.
[121] Luke 18:6.
[122] Bloomberg, *Matthew, supra* at 223.
[123] Luke 18:1.
[124] Luke 18:7.
[125] Luke 18:8.
[126] Crossway Bibles, *The ESV Study Bible* 1994 (2008).
[127] *Sec. & Exch. Comm'n v. Tex. Gulf Sulphur Co.*, 401 F.2d 833 (2d Cir. 1968).
[128] *Id.* at 843.
[129] *Id.*

found a treasure hidden in a field, as in the Parable of the Hidden Treasure, and set about to acquire the field for joy of the treasure contained therein, in this case remarkable mineral deposits including cooper, zinc, and silver.[130] TGS did not disclose this important discovery to the owners of the remainder of the Kid 55 segment before purchasing their land. In fact, TGS took steps to actively conceal the discovery, presumably to buy the land as cheaply as possible.[131] TGS was not condemned for this because, as discussed above, there is no general duty to disclose material nonpublic information before engaging in commercial transactions. TGS knew the real value of the land, the sellers did not, and yet the law did not require that TGS either disclose or abstain from transacting.

However, in addition to the land transactions, several officers, directors, and other TGS insiders (and those tipped by the insiders) (collectively the "insiders") engaged in securities transactions as a result of the discovery.[132] Relying on the material nonpublic information of the ore strike, and anticipating that TGS's stock price was certain to appreciate substantially upon disclosure of the ore strike, the insiders purchased TGS stock and call options.[133] The SEC pursued these insiders for violations of Section 10(b) of the Securities Exchange Act of 1934 and Rule 10b-5 promulgated thereunder.[134]

Unlike the land transactions, where trading on the basis of material nonpublic information is permitted, the securities transactions engaged in by the insiders were found to violate Section 10(b) and Rule 10b-5.[135] The court applied the familiar disclose-or-abstain-from-trading rule in securities regulation, which provides that a person in possession of material nonpublic information, assuming some duty to either the company or the source of the information, must either make public disclosure of the information or refrain from trading until the information is disclosed and, at least in part, assimilated by the market.[136] Therefore, the court concluded that the insiders had violated the law by their trades due to the fact that they were in possession of material nonpublic information when trading.[137]

The comparison between the land transactions and the securities transactions is stark. Trading on material nonpublic information in the land transactions, like most market transactions, is generally held not to violate the law. Just as in the Parable of the Hidden Treasure, there is no general disclose or abstain rule. However, trading on material nonpublic information in the securities markets is, in most cases, considered to be illegal. This is a significant difference from most markets and a significant departure from the

---

[130] *Id.* at 843-844.
[131] *Id.*
[132] *Id.* at 844.
[133] *Id.*
[134] *Id.* at 839-843.
[135] *Id.* at 852.
[136] *Id.* at 848-849. *See also Chiarella, Dirks, and O'Hagan.*
[137] *Id.* at 852.

law of nature and nature's God, which, accordingly, requires some justification. To put it simply, *SEC v. Texas Gulf Sulphur* and the rest of the recently presented materials clearly demonstrate that securities markets are treated quite differently than most other markets. This begs the question: Why treat securities markets so differently?

Judge Posner in *Economic Analysis of Law* doesn't really attempt to explain why financial markets are treated so differently. Rather, he just discusses the relative efficiency of various methods of regulation and notes that a system of disclosure and antifraud does seem to improve the operation of securities markets and therefore presumably their efficiency.

Other secular (and even law and economics) thinkers have offered more reasons. For example, it has been suggested that the importance of the financial markets (as pointed out at the beginning of this chapter) to the individuals and the economy as a whole justifies additional regulation. Further, financials assets such as stocks or bonds are intangible and therefore hard to value accurately such that additional regulation is required. Without some additional evidence of a market failure or the like, these are likely to not be all that persuasive even to many law and economics scholars. Except for the havoc that can be wrought on the whole of society by the markets, the other explanations smack of paternalism.

However, the importance of the markets to society as a whole can be coupled with some additional arguments that make it much more persuasive from a law and economics perspective. Many argue that, due to a market failure, there will not be sufficient information disclosed about financial assets and therefore government intervention beyond the normal is justified. The argument generally runs that investors are widely dispersed and, although they need information, no single investor has the proper incentives to expend the necessary resources to gather the necessary information because any information that he gathers will benefit all investors, at least in part, because if nothing else his trades will communicate his information at least in a general way to the entire market by causing either a rise or fall in prices. This demonstrates both a collective action problem and a free-rider problem. It is suggested by at least some law and economics scholars that government mandated disclosure should be used to solve this market failure.

While that might be persuasive to law and economics thinkers and many others, none of these secular explanations for the heightened regulation of financial markets are appealing from a Christian perspective. The jurisdiction of the civil magistrate is normally not triggered just because there is a market failure or problem or even because something is *really* important. Rather, the proposed activity by the civil magistrate must fit within the biblical jurisdiction of the civil magistrate. Certainly, punishing evildoing, such as fraud, fits squarely within the biblical jurisdiction of the civil government. Requiring disclosure, on the other hand, does not appear to fit. Thus, we are left with two options. Either: (1) the current regime for the regulation of financial markets is biblically unjustified, or (2) there must be some explanation provided that satisfies biblical criteria for governmental action.

II.   Justifying, If Possible, a Higher Level of Civil Government Intervention in the Financial Markets

The following are penultimate, as opposed to ultimate, thoughts on a possible justification for a higher level of civil government intervention in the modern financial markets. I am not entirely sure that I am convinced myself, but I offer it as at least a possible justification for the regulation of securities markets that is consistent with a Christian worldview and a law of nature approach to law.

Limited liability is not a part of the law of nature and nature's God. It is not necessarily contrary to it, though some Christian scholars have argued that it is. For the present, I will assume that it is not. In other words, I will assume that it is not required but it is also not forbidden by the law of nature and nature's God.

That assumption being made, limited liability is a privilege created and granted by the state (the civil magistrate) and our current financial markets absolutely and utterly depend upon it. A quick example will suffice. A number of years ago, General Motors Corporation filed bankruptcy. The common shareholders got virtually nothing, but, they were not required to pay anything either. In other words, their liability was limited—limited to their investment in the company. They lost their investment, but they did not lose any of their personal assets due to the state-granted privilege of limited liability.

What if, on the other hand, there were no limited liability. The creditors of GM, and there were many, could sue the common GM shareholders because they would be jointly and severally liable for GM's debts. If you were a lawyer representing the creditors or the bankruptcy trustee, who would you sue first? The richest shareholder you can find, right? You would hope to recover everything from him, her, or it, and you would let them sort it out with the other shareholders using the right of contribution or the like.

What then would the very rich likely do? Sell all of their public stock holdings, or at least most of them. The risk would simply be too great. Of course, they might own some stock, but it would likely be only in companies they can very effectively oversee and control. Otherwise, again, the risk of losing their entire fortunes would be too great. As they pulled out of the financial markets, the less rich investors would pull out for similar reasons until the capital markets, as we currently know them, collapse.

As noted earlier, the capital markets are enormously important to the world economy. Their collapse would bring disaster around the globe. Therefore, by creating and granting limited liability and limited liability entities, the state has arguably created a very, very dangerous thing.[138] And,

---

[138] This is not to say that it is a bad thing. Some very dangerous things are still good.

when you have a very dangerous thing, like a goring ox or an uncovered pit, you have a duty to protect people and compensate them if they are hurt by it.[139] Accordingly, a heightened level of involvement for the civil magistrate in financial markets could be justified because it is the civil magistrate that created the risky things upon which the financial markets are built. That said, of course, it would still have to be determined what that heightened involvement should look like—perhaps like our current system or perhaps not. And, maybe for that, we should just look for the most efficient system to protect people, assuming that it is not otherwise inconsistent with the law of nature and nature's God.

Notes and Questions

1. What Do You Think? Do you find any of the above explanations or justifications for civil government regulation of financial markets compelling? If so, what should that regulation look like?

2. Are Large Corporations Dangerous? As noted above, the United States financial markets are critical to the entire world's economy. In fact, the vast majority of wealth in America is held by large, publicly-traded corporations. In the following dissenting opinion, Justice Brandies, an early and important proponent of our current system of disclosure and antifraud securities regulation, expresses the opinion that large corporations are dangerous and can be closely regulated by the government. As you read his opinion, consider whether you agree with him? Is the consolidation of wealth in the hands of large corporations and in the financial markets dangerous? Is this a bad thing for freedom? For the economy? For small, closely-held businesses? Or, is Justice Brandies just being an alarmist (which, given that this was written during the throes of the Great Depression, might be understandable)? Also, consider how his arguments might apply to the question of what is the justification for government regulation of the financial markets?

Louis K. Liggett, Co. v. Lee
288 U.S. 517 (1933)

Brandies, J. (dissenting in part) . . . The prevalence of the corporation in America has led men of this generation to act, at times, as if the privilege of doing business in corporate form were inherent in the citizen; and has led them to accept the evils attendant upon the free and unrestricted use of the corporate mechanism as if these evils were the inescapable price of civilized life, and, hence, to be borne with resignation. Throughout the greater part of our history

---

[139] Look back at the Torts chapter in this book for more information on this.

a different view prevailed. Although the value of this instrumentality in commerce and industry was fully recognized, incorporation for business was commonly denied long after it had been freely granted for religious, educational, and charitable purposes. Fear of encroachment upon the liberties and opportunities of the individual. Fear of the subjection of labor to capital. Fear of monopoly. Fear that the absorption of capital by corporations, and their perpetual life, might bring evils similar to those which attended mortmain. There was a sense of some insidious menace inherent in large aggregations of capital, particularly when held by corporations. So at first the corporate privilege was granted sparingly; and only when the grant seemed necessary in order to procure for the community some specific benefit otherwise unattainable. The later enactment of general incorporation laws does not signify that the apprehension of corporate domination had been overcome. The desire for business expansion created an irresistible demand for more charters; and it was believed that under general laws embodying safeguards of universal application the scandals and favoritism incident to special incorporation could be avoided. The general laws, which long embodied severe restrictions upon size and upon the scope of corporate activity, were, in part, an expression of the desire for equality of opportunity.

[Justice Brandies describes the relaxation of requirements imposed upon business corporations. He notes that initially corporations were limited as to size, capital structure, powers, and purpose. He then details how these requirements were, over the years, relaxed.]

. . . Able, discerning scholars have pictured for us the economic and social results of thus removing all limitations upon the size and activities of business corporations and of vesting in their managers vast powers once exercised by stockholders—results not designed by the states and long unsuspected. They show that size alone gives to giant corporations a social significance not attached ordinarily to smaller units of private enterprise. Through size, corporations, once merely an efficient tool employed by individuals in the conduct of private business have become an institution—an institution which has brought such concentration of economic power that so-called private corporations are sometimes able to dominate the state. The typical business corporation of the last century, owned by a small group of individuals, managed by their owners, and limited in size by their personal wealth, is being supplanted by huge concerns in which the lives of tens or hundreds of thousands of employees and the property of tens or hundreds of thousands of investors are subjected, through the corporate mechanism, to the control of a few men. Ownership has been separated from control; and this separation has removed many of the checks which formerly operated to curb the misuse of wealth and power. And, as ownership of the shares is becoming continually more dispersed, the power which formerly accompanied ownership is becoming increasingly concentrated in the hands of a few. The changes thereby wrought in the lives of the workers, of the owners and of the general public, are so fundamental and far-reaching as to lead these scholars to compare the evolving 'corporate system' with the feudal system; and to lead other men of insight and experience to assert that this 'master institution of civilised life' is committing it to the rule of a plutocracy.

The data submitted in support of these conclusions indicate that in the United States the process of absorption has already advanced so far that perhaps two-thirds of our industrial wealth has passed from individual possession to the ownership of large corporations whose shares are dealt in on the stock exchange; that 200 nonbanking corporations, each with assets in excess of $90,000,000, control directly about one-fourth of all our national wealth, and that their influence extends far beyond the assets under their direct control; that these 200 corporations, while nominally controlled by about 2,000 directors, are actually dominated by a few hundred persons—the negation of industrial democracy. Other writers have shown that, coincident with the growth of these giant corporations, there has occurred a marked concentration of individual wealth; and that the resulting disparity in incomes is a major cause of the existing depression. Such is the Frankenstein monster which states have created by their corporation laws.

. . . Among these 200 corporations, each with assets in excess of $90,000,000, are five of the plaintiffs [who were chain stores complaining of a tax in Florida that taxed them more heavily than stores with less locations]. These five have, in the aggregate, $820,000,000 of assets; and they operate, in the several states, an aggregate of 19,718 stores. A single one of these giants operates nearly 16,000. Against these plaintiffs, and other owners of multiple stores, the individual retailers of Florida are engaged in a struggle to preserve their independence—perhaps a struggle for existence. The citizens of the state, considering themselves vitally interested in this seemingly unequal struggle, have undertaken to aid the individual retailers by subjecting the owners of multiple stores to the handicap of higher license fees. They may have done so merely in order to preserve competition. But their purpose may have been a broader and deeper one. They may have believed that the chain store, by furthering the concentration of wealth and of power and by promoting absentee ownership, is thwarting American ideals; that it is making impossible equality of opportunity; that it is converting independent tradesmen into clerks; and that it is sapping the resources, the vigor and the hope of the smaller cities and towns.

. . .

. . . The chain store is treated as a thing menacing the public welfare. The aim of the statute, at the lowest, is to preserve the competition of the independent stores with the chain stores; at the highest, its aim is to eliminate altogether the corporate chain stores from retail distribution. . . .

The plaintiffs discuss the broad question whether the power to tax may be used for the purpose of curbing, or of exterminating, the chain stores by whomsoever owned. It is settled that a state 'may carry out a policy' by 'adjusting its revenue laws and taxing system in such a way as to favor certain industries or forms of industry.' And, since the Fourteenth Amendment 'was not intended to compel the states to adopt an iron rule of equal taxation,' it may exempt from taxation kinds of business which it wishes to promote; and may burden more heavily kinds of business which it wishes to discourage. To do that has been the practice also of the federal government. It protects, by customs duties, our manufacturers and producers from the competition of foreigners. It protects, by the oleomargarine laws, our farmers and dairymen from the competition of other Americans. It eliminated, by a prohibitive tax, the issue of state bank notes in competition with those of national banks. Such is the constitutional power of Congress and of the state Legislatures. The wisdom of its exercise is not the concern of this Court.

. . .

There is a widespread belief that the existing unemployment is the result, in large part, of the gross inequality in the distribution of wealth and income which giant corporations have fostered; that by the control which the few have exerted through giant corporations individual initiative and effort are being paralyzed, creative power impaired and human happiness lessened; that the true prosperity of our past came not from big business, but through the courage, the energy, and the resourcefulness of small men; that only by releasing from corporate control the faculties of the unknown many, only by reopening to them the opportunities for leadership, can confidence in our future be restored and the existing misery be overcome; and that only through participation by the many in the responsibilities and determinations of business can Americans secure the moral and intellectual development which is essential to the maintenance of liberty. If the citizens of Florida share that belief, I know of nothing in the Federal Constitution which precludes the state from endeavoring to give it effect and prevent domination in intrastate commerce by subjecting corporate chains to discriminatory license fees. To that extent, the citizens of each state are still masters of their destiny.

Notes and Questions

1. The Privilege of the Corporate Form. Justice Brandies points out that the privilege of doing business in the corporate form is not inherent in citizenship. Another way to say this might be that the corporation (and indeed the limited liability company and other similar business forms) are created and authorized by the state and are not part of the laws of nature or nature's God, as was indicated earlier in the discussion of limited liability. Since these entities are a creation of the civil government and therefore operating in the corporate form is a privilege, should the civil government be able to regulate them differently than it does a private individual? To state it a bit differently, does the civil magistrate have greater jurisdiction in these areas? Should this include, as Justice Brandies suggests, the power to tax a corporation or class of corporations out of existence? Should it include a robust system of securities regulation, perhaps one even more robust than the one we currently have in the United States? As you should know by now, these questions get at a more fundamental question: from the perspective of a Christian worldview, what is the proper role of the civil government in general and in the economy in particular?[140]

2. Is Limited Liability the Problem? As noted earlier, one of the unique aspects of corporations is that they offer their shareholders limited liability, meaning that the shareholders' liability is limited to their investment in the company. Also as stated earlier, without limited liability, our financial system could not function. All of that said, is limited liability a good thing? Is it a biblical concept? Why or why not?

If limited liability, or limited liability alone, is not the problem, what is? Is it the perpetual existence of the corporation (or the limited liability company) as opposed to the partnership or sole proprietorship? If so, how could that be curtailed?

3. Does the Danger Run Both Ways? God entrusts us with property and expects us to use it for His glory. We have already noted the dangers associated with large corporations and the financial markets. However, does this danger run both ways? In other words, is there a danger in giving the resources that God has entrusted to us to manage for His glory to others to manage for us? Is this shirking our responsibilities to God? Is this like gambling, only a legal version involving something like stocks? Or, is it a way for all of us to share in the profits of various enterprises across the country and around the world?[141]

4. Are Large Corporations and the Financial Markets Composed of them Dangerous? Having considered all of these materials, we can now turn back to the question of whether large corporations and the financial markets composed primarily of them and their securities are dangerous. Certainly large corporations have produced a number of products and technological breakthroughs for which we should be truly thankful. Consider, for instance, the computer on which this book was typed. Or, think of the many life-saving medical treatments that we have. Most of these things were developed and mass-produced by large corporations. Further, large corporations employ literally millions of people. And, of course, the large corporations rely on the highly developed financial markets to fund these efforts.

However, abuses in large corporations and the financial markets have caused much pain and suffering. In the Enron scandal, many people lost enormous amounts of money. Some lost their entire retirement savings. In addition, the Great Recession was triggered, in part, by abuses in the investment and home mortgage industry. (Consider the question about the role of government in relation to this last sentence. Did the Federal Government's earlier interventions in the housing market play a role in the later financial disaster?)

---

[140] *See* Romans 13:1-7; 1 Peter 2:13-17; Bern, *Biblical Model* 116-131 (1995).
[141] *See* Ecclesiastes 11:1; Matthew 25:14-30; and Luke 19:11-27.

After reading the opinion of Justice Brandies and considering the preceding questions, Scriptures, and other materials, what do you think? Are large corporations dangerous? What about the current financial markets? Should they be illegal? Closely regulated? Are they consistent with a Christian worldview? If not, what alternative system would you offer? If they are consistent with a Christian worldview, do you think there are abuses about which Christians should be concerned? If so, whose jurisdiction is it to address those abuses and how should they be addressed? How would Judge Posner answer these questions?

Many people in our society today take it as a given that inequality in wealth or income is a bad thing. It is not a question of whether inequality is bad for these folks (because they start with the assumption that it is bad), but rather to them the question is merely what is to be done about it. This is a classic example of assuming something that one should prove.

Judge Posner, arguing from a law and economics perspective, doesn't appear to be convinced that inequality is "bad," which to him would not be a very meaningful term unless by that you mean "inefficient." He seems to conclude that it is generally not inefficient unless it becomes so extreme that it threatens stability in society. He spends a good deal of time discussing the options available for alleviating or lessening wealth and/or income inequality, but he does not appear to be convinced that it is necessarily a goal society should pursue.[142]

From a Christian perspective, the answer may be quite shocking. I would argue that the answer is that inequality is not only not a bad thing, but it is actually a good thing—it is a gracious gift from God providing us with many opportunities to glorify Him. That certainly doesn't mean that a Christian should not be concerned about the poor—on the contrary, *The Bible* is full of warnings to be gracious and generous to the poor.[143] A Christian should very much be concerned about poor people, but it does not follow that this is necessarily an issue for law and policy. Rather, based upon the principles of the limited jurisdiction of the civil magistrate discussed elsewhere in this book, it seems to be primarily an issue for the family, the church, or the individual, while the civil magistrate seems to primarily be involved by providing justice, to the poor as well as the rich.

---

[142] However, I am not convinced that he thinks it is a goal society should not pursue either. He does here seem to really take an explanatory position. He seems to be merely trying to predict which programs are likely to be effective if the goal is to ameliorate wealth and/or income inequality and nothing more.

[143] The number of verses that could be cited here is staggering. Here is a sample: Exodus 22:22, 23:6 and 11; Leviticus 19:10 and 15; Deuteronomy 24:17; Proverbs 14:31; Jeremiah 2:34 and 5:28; Ezekiel 22:29; Amos 4:1 and 8:4-6; Matthew 25:39-40; Acts 2:45 and 4:35; Galatians 2:10; Titus 3:14: and 1 John 3:17. Note, however, that none of these verses command the civil magistrate to undertake a course of action to alleviate poverty, other than preventing oppression and providing equal justice.

Dr. Wayne Grudem, in his excellent book *Business for the Glory of God*, has a compelling chapter on this issue that I would highly recommend to you. In summing the chapter up, he writes:

> [T]he New Testament emphasis on helping the poor shows us that there is an extreme kind of inequality that is not good, a point where people are in poverty and should be helped. (Just what "poverty" is will vary from society to society and will also vary over time within any one society.) [Dr. Grudem had earlier noted that "[p]overty is one of the results of living in a world affected by sin and the Fall."]
>
> * * * In contrast to many admonitions to help the poor, there is no corresponding command in the New Testament to take some wealth away from the very rich, and there is no teaching that a large amount of wealth is wrong in itself. [Dr. Grudem then notes that the wealthy are subject to additional temptation and may succumb to those temptations by using their wealth in ways that are not God-honoring.]
>
> * * *
>
> But, the distortions of something good must not cause us to think that the thing itself is evil. The evils of poverty and excessive, self-indulgent wealth must not cause us to think that God's goal is total equality of possessions, or that all inequalities are wrong. Inequalities in abilities and opportunities and possessions will be part of our life in heaven forever, and they are in themselves good and pleasing to God, and provide many opportunities for glorifying him.[144]

Whether or not one agrees with Dr. Grudem as to the goodness of a certain level of inequality, for the purposes of this chapter and considering inequality as an issue of law and policy for the civil magistrate to address, we only need conclude that it is not evil rising to the level of *kakos* in order for it to be outside the jurisdiction of the civil magistrate and therefore left to some of the other jurisdictions created by God.[145] That said, let's consider some of the arguments supporting the idea that wealth and income inequality are actually good gifts from God (and therefore certainly not within the jurisdiction of the civil magistrate). We will begin by considering the eternal state.

We can know that inequality is not a sin or morally wrong because there will be inequality in the eternal state and there can be no sin or anything morally wrong in the eternal state. *See, e.g.,* Revelation 21:27. The Parable of the Minas demonstrates this point. It reads:

---

[144] Grudem, *Business for the Glory of God* 57-60 (2003).
[145] For more information on the jurisdiction of the civil magistrate and its limitations, see the discussion earlier in the Contracts chapter on that topic.

[11] As they heard these things, he proceeded to tell a parable, because he was near to Jerusalem, and because they supposed that the kingdom of God was to appear immediately. [12] He said therefore, "A nobleman went into a far country to receive for himself a kingdom and then return. [13] Calling ten of his servants, he gave them ten minas, and said to them, 'Engage in business until I come.' [14] But his citizens hated him and sent a delegation after him, saying, 'We do not want this man to reign over us.' [15] When he returned, having received the kingdom, he ordered these servants to whom he had given the money to be called to him, that he might know what they had gained by doing business. [16] The first came before him, saying, 'Lord, your mina has made ten minas more.' [17] And he said to him, 'Well done, good servant! Because you have been faithful in a very little, you shall have authority over ten cities.' [18] And the second came, saying, 'Lord, your mina has made five minas.' [19] And he said to him, 'And you are to be over five cities.' [20] Then another came, saying, 'Lord, here is your mina, which I kept laid away in a handkerchief; [21] for I was afraid of you, because you are a severe man. You take what you did not deposit, and reap what you did not sow.' [22] He said to him, 'I will condemn you with your own words, you wicked servant! You knew that I was a severe man, taking what I did not deposit and reaping what I did not sow? [23] Why then did you not put my money in the bank, and at my coming I might have collected it with interest?' [24] And he said to those who stood by, 'Take the mina from him, and give it to the one who has the ten minas.' [25] And they said to him, 'Lord, he has ten minas!' [26] 'I tell you that to everyone who has, more will be given, but from the one who has not, even what he has will be taken away. [27] But as for these enemies of mine, who did not want me to reign over them, bring them here and slaughter them before me.' "[146]

Accordingly, based upon the foregoing, it seems clear that there will be inequality in the eternal state with some people having far greater authority than others. This idea is supported as well by a number of passages in *The Bible* on the final judgment, which indicate that some people will receive more rewards than others based upon their actions in this life.[147] Wayne Grudem notes that these passages "imply *degrees of reward* for what we have done in

---

[146] Luke 19:11-27 (ESV).

[147] *See, e.g.,* 1 Corinthians 3:12-15, 4:5; 2 Corinthians 5:10. *See also* Grudem, *Business for the Glory of God* 53-60, 86 n. 1 (2003).

this life" and that therefore some level of inequality must be a good thing given that it will exist in the eternal state.[148]

Second, as Wayne Grudem also notes, "[e]ven among the angels, there are differing levels of authority and stewardship established by God, and therefore we cannot say that such a system is wrong or sinful in itself."[149] For example, Michael is referred to as an Archangel in *Jude* 9 and a chief prince in *Daniel* 10:13. Further, other ranks, orders, positions, or levels of authority and responsibility are suggested by passages such as *Psalm* 89:5, 7, *Ephesians* 3:10 and 6:12, and 1 *Peter* 3:22. God is clearly the creator of and organizer of these beings, and it is He who has given them their varying ranks, authorities, and responsibilities. Inequality is inherent in this, and, therefore, inequality cannot be said to be evil in and of itself.

Third, we see in the world a great variety or inequality of God-given talents, abilities, and inheritances. These inequalities naturally lead to inequalities in income, wealth, and possessions. For example, the heir or heiress to a major fortune was chosen by God to be born into the family. Her birth has all but guaranteed her greater wealth and possessions than the vast majority of other people. Another example would be professional athletes. No matter how hard I try or train, I am incapable of dunking a basketball. Yet, some people are born with great aptitudes for sports, which enable them to make very large incomes as professional athletes. Or consider someone exceptionally gifted in invention or leadership. He or she will almost certainly be rewarded with greater income and possessions based upon the cultivation and exercise of these natural abilities. And, of course, someone born into a family that cares about his or her education and equipping will undoubtedly have advantages that will lead to more income and possessions.

Surely it is God who has given these unequal abilities (and starting places or opportunities) out, and God cannot be said to have behaved unjustly in so doing because He is the standard of justice. Wayne Grudem writes that these "[i]nequalities are necessary in a world that requires a great variety of tasks to be done." He continues:

> Some tasks require stewardship of large amounts of resources (such as ownership of a steel mill or a company that manufactures airplanes), and some tasks require stewardship of small amounts of resources. And God has given some people greater abilities than others, abilities in artistic or musical skills, abilities in mathematics or science, abilities in leadership, abilities in business skills and buying and selling, and so forth. If reward for each person's labor is given fairly and is based on the value of what that person produces, then those with larger abilities will naturally gain larger rewards. Since people are different in abilities and effort, I don't think

---

[148] Grudem, *Business for the Glory of God* 52.
[149] *Id.*

there could be a fair system of rewards for work unless the system had different rewards for different people. Fairness of reward requires such differences.[150]

It is clear that God has built inequality of stewardship, possessions, responsibilities, etc. into this world, the angelic realm, and the world to come. It can therefore hardly be said that inequality in and of itself is wrong. Rather, it must be concluded that such a thing, clearly given from God, is in fact a good gift that, like many others, is subject to perversion but remains good nonetheless.[151]

Notes and Questions

1. What do you think? Do you think that inequality of wealth and income is a bad thing? A good thing? What are the implications for law and public policy regarding the answer to this question?

2. Role of the Civil Magistrate in Fighting Poverty? What do you think the role of the civil magistrate in redistributing wealth and fighting poverty should be? To help you answer these materials, refer back to Chapter 3 and the discussion of jurisdiction there. Also, you would likely be greatly helped by reviewing Professor Bern's excellent article quoted in that chapter. In discussing two related issues, public education and the National Endowment for the Arts, Professor Bern writes:

> Under the Model analysis, Civil Government is acting beyond its jurisdiction when it establishes and operates [public] schools. In doing so, it is not functioning within its acknowledged jurisdiction to punish evildoers, to prevent evildoing, or to provide for redress for harm caused by evildoing. With the exception of its jurisdiction to commend those who do well, Civil Government's realm of authority is clearly coercive in nature. That is reflected even in the manner in which it obtains funding for its authorized functions—by taxation, a compulsory assessment, as contrasted with the manner in which private institutions obtain resources for their activities.

---

[150] *Id.*

[151] *The Bible* is clear that the rich face greater temptations due to their possessions. *See, e.g.,* 1 Timothy 6:9. However, *The Bible* does not indicate that the rich have a monopoly on greed or that they are in sin merely because they are rich. See for example, Abraham, Isaac, Jacob, Solomon, Barnabas, Lydia, Philemon, and many others. All appear to have been very rich, and none are condemned for merely being rich. Thus, the fact that rich people face great temptations, but are not in fact in sin for merely being rich, tends to also support the fact that some level of inequality of wealth or income is not in and of itself evil.

* * * The Scripture is clear, however, that parents have been given jurisdiction and the command to teach their children. Parents may carry out their responsibility to educate their children in a variety of ways, including joining together with other parents to establish private schools to do so. Whatever the means selected, however, the responsibility is one which the parents cannot abdicate. The Church has also been given jurisdiction and the command to teach the truth.

Might it be said that Civil Government is commending those who do well when it provides government education? Not under the Model analysis. First, it must be underscored that the doing well which is to be commended is that of others (i.e. those outside the institution of Civil Government), and that under the Model there is no roving commission for Civil Government itself to do well in the abstract. Recall that under the Model, the jurisdiction of Civil Government is defined in its relation to the other jurisdictions and not in some freestanding, independent way.

* * *

Two other observations should be made, which may help cushion the initial shock caused by what might be termed the Model's counter-intuitive conclusion regarding public education. First, recall that stewardship-dominion duties include the phase of giving. Consider the benefits that could accrue if Civil Government did not tax to support its schools. Individuals, families, and the voluntary associations they might form would have additional resources over which to exercise authority. Consistent with effective stewardship principles, they might well choose to express love those who have less by providing scholarship assistance or other assistance to aid them in educating their children.

The Church as well might find new opportunities (and challenges) to really operate fully as the Church, that is, to be an instrument of love and assistance to those endeavoring to carry out their duties of educating their children.

The second observation is pragmatic. There is no reason to believe that an entity which is attempting to perform a function outside of the authority conferred upon it is likely to do it well. In fact, in the case of public education, the "proof is in the pudding" test appears to be strong confirmation of the Model's conclusion that education is not within the jurisdiction of Civil Government.

* * *

Under the Model analysis, Civil Government is not acting within its jurisdiction when it does so. What has just been said regarding its taxing to support government schools is also applicable here. It is obviously not acting within its jurisdiction to punish evildoing, to prevent evildoing, or to provide for redress for harm caused by the same.

Can it be said that it is appropriately acting in its "commending those who do well" authority? Is there anything inherently different in the activity of one who, for example, paints or sculpts or dances, and that of one who practices medicine or builds bridges or works as a plumber? It cannot be doubted that elements of skill and creativity are involved in every stewardship-dominion activity from which one might produce income for the needs of life. In terms of an individual's "doing well," it is not self-evident that there is an inherent difference between doing an activity in the "fine arts" or in the "useful arts" or in other productive endeavors.

A difference which does appear to exist between the activities mentioned is the nature and extent of the demand for them. Activities illustrated by the examples in the first category or the products produced by them have aesthetic appeal. The appeal to taste holds the potential for great financial gain if one can create something which, in turn, creates great aesthetic appeal in another who is able and willing to pay money to satisfy that appeal. But because its appeal is to taste, instead of to functional needs, the market in which to sell is more limited.

However, this difference is not unique between the categories. It exists within the categories as well. There may be a larger market for the services of a plumber than for those of a bridge builder. Because of specialties or geographic location, there may be a larger market for one physician than for another in terms of potential buyers of their services.

Taxing by Civil Government, and payments by it to make up for these economic realities, accomplishes a redistribution of income by Civil Government. This is perhaps a reflection of the belief that Civil Government itself should make up for any harsh economic realities. This belief, however, does not thereby transform such activity into the realm of "commending" those who do well. From what has been said with regard to the public education issue, it is also clear that this income redistribution to accomplish a function which is not within the jurisdiction of Civil Government improperly interferes with the stewardship-dominion duties of those taxed.[152]

---

[152] Bern, *Biblical Model* 174-179.

Based upon the foregoing analysis of public education and the National Endowment for the Arts, what do you think Professor Bern would have concluded about taxing people in order to redistribute wealth and reduce wealth and income inequality? What do you think? Is it within the role of the civil magistrate?

3. New Testament Socialism or Communism? At times, people have attempted to argue that the New Testament actually changed much of the discussion above because it endorses a type of ecclesiastical socialism or communism. The primary citation is usually to the book of Acts. From this, they argue in varying degrees that private property rights should be abandoned and/or the civil government should take an active and coercive role in alleviating poverty and redistributing wealth in the New Testament era. The relevant passage is Acts 2:41-47(ESV). It reads:

> And they devoted themselves to the apostles' teaching and the fellowship, to the breaking of bread and the prayers. And awe came upon every soul, and many wonders and signs were being done through the apostles. And all who believed were together and had all things in common. And they were selling their possessions and belongings and distributing the proceeds to all, as any had need. And day by day, attending the temple together and breaking bread in their homes, they received their food with glad and generous hearts, praising God and having favor with all the people. And the Lord added to their number day by day those who were being saved.

Despite these assertions by some, this is not a communistic or socialistic situation, and it does not argue for the abolition of private property rights or the forcible redistribution of wealth. First, it assumes private property rights. If there were no private property rights, they could not be selling *their* (note the possessive pronoun) possessions. In fact, the very words "possessions" and "belongings" indicate ownership.

Second, the situation in Acts 2 was clearly voluntary. The civil government was not forcing the believers to part with their property, nor was the early church. For one to generously give of one's own positions to meet the needs of others or to support the work of the church is a laudable thing. That was what was occurring here in Acts 2. However, for the civil government to use the coercive power of the sword to take from some to give to others is stealing and wicked, unless of course it is within the limited jurisdiction given to the civil government by God. The difference between socialism, communism, and other modern civil-government-led redistribution projects and what was occurring in the early church is the difference between voluntarily disposing of one's own property and being forced to part with one's property by the threat of the sword of the civil government.

Further, the story of Ananias and Sapphira in Acts 5 illustrates very clearly that the point is not the abolition of private property rights and/or forced redistribution of wealth, but rather the generosity of the early church. Ananias and Sapphira, apparently envious of the recognition that some were getting for their generosity, chose to sell some property they owned. However, they wickedly decided to withhold some while indicating that they had given it all. Peter's rebuke to Ananias in Acts 5:3-4 demonstrates that deception and lying to the Holy Spirit was the problem.

> But Peter said, "Ananias, why has Satan filled your heart to lie to the Holy Spirit and to keep back for yourself part of the proceeds of the land? While it remained unsold, did it not remain your own? And after it was sold, was it not at your disposal? Why is it that you have contrived this deed in your heart? You have not lied to men but to God." (emphasis added)

Peter's statements assume private property rights and clearly state that the giving in the early church was voluntary, not compulsory. While Ananias owned it, it belonged to him, not to everyone, no one, the civil government, or the church. After he sold it, the proceeds similarly belonged to him. Thus, the situation of the early church cannot be used to support socialism, communism, forced redistribution of wealth by the civil magistrate, or the abolition of private property rights.

4. Is there an answer? Jesus said that there would always be poor among us.[153] Accordingly, any war on poverty or the like seems doomed to failure. However, God has given means by which the suffering of extreme poverty may be eliminated. One method is through charity and generosity conducted by churches, families, and individuals, whose jurisdictions do very much include voluntary giving to the poor.

Another very important method is business and commercial activity. Of this, Dr. Grudem writes:

> I believe *the only long-term solution to world poverty is business.* That is because businesses produce goods, and businesses produce jobs. And businesses continue producing goods year after year, and continue producing jobs and paying wages year after year. Therefore if we are ever going to see *long-term* solutions to world poverty, I believe it will come through starting and maintaining productive, profitable businesses.[154]

Business and commercial activity, justly conducted, benefits all of society. Or, as John F. Kennedy purportedly said, a rising tide lifts all ships. We see this

---

[153] Matthew 26:11, Mark 14:7, and John 12:8.
[154] Grudem, *Business for the Glory of God* 80-81 (emphasis in original).

in our society today. Even the poor among us frequently enjoy things that Nebuchadnezzar, Cyrus, or Caesar Augustus, certainly very rich men, would have given half their kingdoms for, such as cars (automated chariots that run on small, controlled explosions), air conditioning, cellular telephones, or television. In many ways, virtually all of us in modern American are very rich by the standards of history, but that wealth has almost exclusively come through business and commercial activity.

What then is the civil government's role in this? It does have one, and it is critical. It is to provide an environment of justice for all, poor and rich alike, including the enforcement of contracts and freedom to contract, the protection of private property rights, the avoidance of unnecessary interference with and restrictions on entrepreneurship and business activity, and the avoidance of giving out special favors or privileges, especially to large corporations and businesses (often called "crony capitalism" or "corporate welfare.") Where the civil government acts in this restrained way, i.e., within its proper jurisdiction, the potential of ordinary people is set free, and that potential has a way of working itself out through business and commercial activity to the benefit of all.[155]

---

[155] *See, e.g.,* Grudem, *Business for the Glory of God*; Grudem and Asmus, *The Poverty of Nations*; and Hernando de Soto, *The Mystery of Capital: Why Capitalism Triumphs in the West and Fails Everywhere Else* (2000).